Jamie Jauncey is one of Scotland'
written word and of clear commun
English equivalent. They have much
121 with a remarkable light touch.

Author of The No 1

Business writing — at its best — invites a conversation between
the company and its customer; John and Jamie show how that
conversational process works as each builds on the other's words.
Two of the most engaging, encouraging and entertaining experts
in their field, share their wisdom with charm, generosity of spirit
and a seriousness of purpose.

Andy Milligan,
Author and brand expert

John Simmons and Jamie Jauncey have that rare gift of the very
best teachers: they help people discover talents they never knew
they had. If you want to be led on an exhilarating journey into
the creative possibilities of language, you couldn't hope to find
better guides.

Tom Scott,
Senior Lecturer, MA Professional Writing,
University College Falmouth

If I had several lives I'd want at least one of them to consist of hanging
around and working with the likes of Simmons and Jauncey.

Richard Pelletier,
Professional writer, Portland, Oregon USA

Copyright © 2011 John Simmons and Jamie Jauncey
Cover design: OpalWorks Pte Ltd

Published in 2011 by Marshall Cavendish Business
An imprint of Marshall Cavendish International

PO Box 65829, London EC1P 1NY, United Kingdom
info@marshallcavendish.co.uk

and

1 New Industrial Road, Singapore 536196
genrefsales@sg.marshallcavendish.com
www.marshallcavendish.com/genref

Other Marshall Cavendish offices: Marshall Cavendish Corporation. 99 White
Plains Road, Tarrytown NY 10591-9001, USA • Marshall Cavendish International
(Thailand) Co Ltd. 253 Asoke, 12th Flr, Sukhumvit 21 Road, Klongtoey Nua,
Wattana, Bangkok 10110, Thailand • Marshall Cavendish (Malaysia) Sdn Bhd. Times
Subang, Lot 46, Subang Hi-Tech Industrial Park, Batu Tiga, 40000 Shah Alam,
Selangor Darul Ehsan, Malaysia

Marshall Cavendish is a trademark of Times Publishing Limited

A CIP record for this book is available from the British Library

ISBN 978-981-4328-59-3

Printed and bound in Great Britain by
TJ International Ltd, Padstow, Cornwall

ROOM 121

JOHN SIMMONS and JAMIE JAUNCEY

A masterclass
in writing and communication
in business

This book is dedicated to all the Dark Angels,
present and future.

*People who write obscurely are either
unskilled in writing or up to mischief.*

**Sir Peter Medawar
(Biologist and Nobel Prize winner)**

CONTENTS

INTRODUCTION

If the bottom line in business is money, the heart and soul of every transaction is a conversation. If it's only money that is exchanged there's no real human connection. And our lives are the poorer for it. For most of us, from our early 20s through to our mid 60s, a third to a half of our lives is spent at work. Can we afford, spiritually and emotionally — even mentally — to simply serve the bottom line?

I learnt a lot about the pleasure of the market place from my father. Portly, indeed once mistaken for King Farouk of Egypt, he was a bit like the bare-breasted Buddha in the Tenth Bull of Zen: 'Barefooted and naked of breast, I mingle with the people of the world. My clothes are ragged and dust-laden, and I am ever blissful. … I visit the wine shop and the market, and everyone I look upon becomes enlightened.'

Dad, who worked for the British Foreign & Commonwealth Office (FCO), was actually quite a dapper dresser, so on that score he departs from similarities with the sage, but in all else he realised that commerce is the currency of human connection outside of family, romance and school. It provides the everyday opportunity to engage and converse and enjoy. It's not just about bars of soap and chicken feed, insurance policies and sachets of nails.

He loved to tell me and my brothers of his visits to his Chinese launderer-come-tailor in Kuala Lumpur. These could have amounted to simple collections of his canvas sack marked with his Pythagorean ID. But no, without fail he would take a bottle of whisky, sit down and chat a while over a dram or two, before negotiating the price for this month's laundry, darned socks or suit and shirt repairs. Years later, as a mischievous elder, he was still at it, regaling the shopkeepers down Glastonbury High Street, with my devoted mother in tow. They may have come away with 10% off here or an extra loaf of bread stuffed in the bakery bag there, but that was not really the point. The point was connection. The alternative is actually pretty deadly: automation and alienation. This is serious stuff, sociologically, not mere nice-to-have frills.

These days, that is what all savvy brands want to do: connect. How? By having a conversation with their customers and potential customers. And what is conversation but imagination, story, twist, embellishment and language carrying along the facts/information/data.

But you can't have all that in business communications. Who said? Which Ayatollah of Industry? *Shrugs all round.* Which Commercial Wizard? Henry Ford? Steve Jobs? Anita Roddick? *General laughter.*

It was through the shared belief in the role of storytelling in the conversation between brand and consumer that I came into contact first with John Simmons and then Jamie Jauncey. All longish in the tooth, and mischievous, but not as elderly as my pops in Avalon, we set about creating a vehicle to share our belief and provide the tools and highly subversive permissions to bring this humansing influence more staunchly into the world of business. The name of the vehicle was (and is and hopefully will continue to be) Dark Angels. And what began as an experiment has turned into an imaginatively graded learning over three levels in three distinct locations. And which, for the ambitious copywriter, isn't a nice-to-have with frills, but a pukka roadmap to a bankable destination. From nowhere to head of verbal identity, from publisher to bestselling author, from marketing assistant to D&AD Yellow Pencil winner — these are just some of our achievements along the way. Because the pen, well wielded, carves a path of enchantment as much in business as in poetry and fiction.

So, I know these guys pretty well. Over the last seven years, we've spent the best part of 2000 hours together playing the role of 'animateur', espousing the use of metaphor, refereeing 'jargon bust' and setting the kind of briefs David Ogilvy would have sacrificed his pipe for.

Room 121 gives you a glimpse of some of the territory we cover in Dark Angels, but roams far beyond the courses' confines, too. It is very much like eavesdropping into a conversation between two writers who treat the subject of writing for business with both the seriousness and lightness of touch it deserves. As I said earlier, business is not the be all and end all but it represents quite a thick wad of what's in between.

This conversation came about because a couple of years ago both John and Jamie embraced the new social network platforms and started writing blogs: John through his '26 Fruits' platform and Jamie through his 'Few Kind Words'. (I, the youngest of the three, lag far behind with my take-up of such platforms, but I'm working on it — watch the ether.)

So the conceit is this: a correspondence formed of one-to-one blogs, batting to and fro across the airwaves from rural Perthshire to London (and from other locations, too, in their peripatetic itineraries), written over the course of a calendar year. At the heart of the correspondence is their belief in the humanising power of language within business and this is illustrated and touched upon through stories from workshops, from jobs, from books, from thinking, from experience — whether travelling or at home.

This is not a debate. The two writers are agreed on the core premise. But neither are they ciphers for a consensual idea. There are subtle nuances to their separate take on the subject. And the source of their insights is their experience, which of course, is individual and unique. So the delight of these exchanges is the richness and variety of anecdote: from how Apollo turned a crow from white to black to riding on horseback across Argentina; from the question 'Why read fiction?' to a visit to the dream chamber at Pergamon; from treating the imagination as a muscle to the blinder from the Tabasco trolley boy; from the tale of a man with a fork in a world of soup to John's mantra, 'constraints liberate'.

Blogs are very much of the moment but most wouldn't get published. These have because they're of substance and well crafted and up until now have constituted a private correspondence. We'll be the richer for their sharing. To me, they're more like essays or meditations in blog form. As ever, it's the message, not the medium, that is of ultimate worth. Now, they're my pals and colleagues, so naturally I'm very pro, but for my money — and hopefully for yours, too, since you've bought the book — these guys are the Montaigne and Plutarch of the modern business world. Enjoy; take heed; pass on.

Stuart Delves
February 2011

Part 1

WINTER

Week 1
John to Jamie

ROOM 121

What is Room 121? Where is it? I guess we should set out what we mean. We're both writers. We write for business but we also write in other ways. We both believe that writing in different forms, such as novels and poetry, makes you a better writer for business. It's a matter of engaging your heart *and* your mind. A lot of business writing fails to engage the hearts and minds of the reader and the writer. Corporate-speak is the result.

But it needn't be so. You can produce writing in a corporate context that makes a human connection. You simply have to write one-to-one, reaching out as one human being talking to another human being, not as one organisation sending information to another organisation. 'Business-to-business' is a well-worn phrase that immediately sets the wrong expectation.

So, as we write to each other through these exchanges, we know that we are writing one-to-one, me to you, you to me. In doing so, we'll explore what makes us the writers we are. And we'll discuss what really works when you, the reader, are writing for business, giving you tips, ideas and practical advice to make your communication more effective.

This means we share a space. It's a space where you go to find new and better ways to write in the business environment. As you've now arrived at our reception, we'll direct you to join us in that space. Let's meet there, it's just along the corridor, in Room 121.

121 THINGS TO DO

With each exchange we'll set you a challenge. We might simply ask you to think about a writing principle — for example, writing one-to-one. If you think this through in relation to your own business writing, where does it take you? Your first exercise is to give directions to the next business meeting you arrange.

Explain as clearly and simply as possible without using a map. But make it sound inviting, unmissable.

Jamie to John

ROOM 101

As you walk down our corridor, you may find yourself thinking that Room 121 has a strangely familiar ring to it. If so, there's a reason.

It's a deliberate echo of George Orwell's novel, *Nineteen Eighty-Four*, and the sinister Room 101 where opponents of Big Brother and the ruling party are tortured by being confronted with their worst fears. In the case of the main character, Winston Smith, that happens to be a cage of hungry rats strapped to his face.

But why would we want the title of our book to set up such a terrible association? Because *Nineteen Eighty-Four* is the story of a society controlled by language, and we see certain obvious parallels with the modern business world.

We're not saying that today's organisations actively seek to control people through the way they speak — at least not the majority of them. But the default setting for so much of what's written and said in the 21st century workplace is a strange half-language that has very little that's really human about it.

Orwell's fictional Newspeak set out to prevent people from expressing and being themselves. Modern corporate-speak just doesn't leave room for it. And as writers, that's something we instinctively react against. Writing has to have personality, otherwise it simply doesn't work — which, as you've already explained, John, is where the one-to-one comes in. We know that Room 121 is infinitely preferable to Room 101.

So our book is about bringing more of ourselves to what we write at work, and the reference to Room 101 is a warning, admittedly rather a dire one, of what might happen if we don't.

You could say we're the Winston Smiths of business writing. But without the rats. Oh, and Big Brother won't get us in the end.

120 THINGS TO DO

'It was a bright cold day in April, and the clocks were striking thirteen.' That's the opening line of George Orwell's *Nineteen Eighty-Four*. Make your own list of great opening lines in novels. Then look at the opening lines of the last 10 business communications you've received. Think about how you might improve them.

Week 2
John to Jamie

BEGINNINGS

A New Year. Look out of the window. Does your heart sink or soar? A new book. My heart soars but what about the reader's? At the start of a new year we're starting this dialogue in words and about words, a book about writing. How better to begin than with some thoughts about beginnings?

Let's start by opening up three books I'd been given for Christmas and reading the opening lines. Here they are:

The truth is, if old Major Dover hadn't dropped dead at Taunton races Jim would never have come to Thursgood's at all.

John le Carré,
Tinker, Tailor, Soldier, Spy

On a dull day in the early 1990s, I took the number 13 bus to Hendon, got off at the corner of Shirehall Lane and walked along it towards the house where I was born.

Oliver Postgate,
Seeing Things

The young Canadian, who could not have been more than fifteen, had hesitated too long.

John Irving,
Last Night in Twisted River

None of them is going to make it to that list of classic first sentences. But each of them is intriguing, each establishes straightaway a tone of voice, and each of them is an invitation to read on. They do it not by telling you a mass of crucial facts, but by tempting you with the suggestion of information that's withheld.

Le Carré starts with the death of a character who will play no part in the story and with lots of questions raised in the reader's mind. That will continue; it's the nature of the spy thriller genre. Oliver Postgate (author of children's books such as *Bagpuss, Noggin, The Clangers*) sends you strolling comfortably back down a road to childhood, to a familiar feeling in an unfamiliar setting that we all still recognise from our own life stories. John Irving leaves you wondering about consequences. What happened as a result of the hesitation? You won't have to wait long to find out; there's already a momentum in the storytelling.

So what should we take from these examples? We can all learn techniques from other writers. Writers of fiction know they have to grab readers from the opening lines. It's true for fiction. It's even more true for business writing. Your business readers probably won't have made the personal commitment of paying their own money to buy your writing. So you need to work hard to get them to read on.

119 THINGS TO DO

It's worth giving a disproportionate amount of attention to the first words of any business communication. It might be an e-mail header or the first sentence of a policy document. How will you begin? Try questions. Write down 10 questions that will really grab your reader.

HANDY WORDS

I sometimes work in my local library. On the walls of its café are quotations about literature and writing from famous literary figures. There's one by Goethe that often catches my eye: 'When ideas fail, words come in very handy.'

The first time I saw it I was confused. What are words if not the expression of ideas? But then I started to think about an exercise that's well known to teachers of creative writing and that we often use in business writing, too. Sometimes known as automatic writing (though I try and avoid the expression — it makes me think of séances), it involves writing continuously, in longhand, on a given subject for three or four minutes.

At its best it produces a stream of consciousness, unfettered by the remembrance of rules or the anticipation of readership; and the results are often surprising. Goethe was right — the simple act of putting words down on the page, one after the other, fast and with as little thought as possible, becomes a kind of lubricant for the imagination.

It can work on a purely personal level, unlocking memories and emotions, but it can also work creatively as a way of getting at trapped or unrealised ideas. And in the world of work, where the prospect of a report, or even an e-mail, can sometimes seem impossibly daunting, a few minutes letting your thoughts flow freely onto paper, safe in the knowledge that no one else will read them, can be a wonderful way of priming the creative, or even simply the narrative, pump.

118 THINGS TO DO

The act of writing makes us think. Your brain might feel empty of thoughts but it won't be if you write. Pick even the most mind-numbing of business subjects — let's say 'pensions'. Now write non-stop for 10 minutes, no editing as you go, just stream-of-consciousness, automatic writing for your eyes only. See what has emerged. There might just be one insight, one good phrase, but that's a good start. It might be the phrase to build your article around.

Week 3

John to Jamie

THE END OF THE BEGINNING

What is a beginning for? To start you reading towards the end.

I wondered how fresh the beginnings might be in the writing for some of our biggest corporations as we enter the new century's second decade. If, for example, I were looking for a change of career, how would I be persuaded to apply to join a big company? So I went to three websites, not knowing what I might find. Here they are:

Sony Ericsson
Energising people's experiences
We want our employees to experience a career with us as being both satisfying and lucrative — because we believe this leads to our collective accomplishments.

Microsoft
Imagine
You have unique experiences, skills and passions — and we believe you can bring them all to Microsoft for a rich, rewarding career and lifestyle that will surprise you with its breadth and potential.

HSBC
If you like working with customers face-to-face, you might be well suited to a role in our retail network, providing

local customers with the kind of excellent service that will help drive the profitability of your branch.

Intrigued? Enticed? Persuaded? I thought not. The problem is that the business community does not learn from good writers outside its own world. It sees the two as unconnected, and that's a big mistake.

As a result the corporation thinks only of its own agenda, rather than asking 'How can we intrigue people enough to read on?' So the corporation writes introductory sentences that try to cram as much information into the opening lines as possible. It comes up with long sentences that repel rather than invite. (Long sentences can work if they are well-constructed to reinforce the meaning of the words — see the Oliver Postgate sentence in *Week 2*).

But it's not as if the information crammed in is all worthwhile. The 39-word opening sentence from HSBC might be rewritten more simply and honestly thus: 'Do you like talking to people? You could help our customers, and you could help your branch make money. '

The opening sentence is so important because it helps the reader to decide. How do I feel about this business? Should I read on? It's worth thinking hard about how you can best do that. It might be by not trying to say too much, just enough to arouse interest.

117 THINGS TO DO
Think about this — look back at the opening sentences of recent pieces you've written at work. Ask yourself: how would I have felt as a reader? Rewrite the openings that don't intrigue or interest even you.

A WORD FROM THE BISHOP

It was how St John opened his Gospel, though Goethe might equally well have said it: 'In the beginning was the word…' But neither of them went on to address the perennial writer's question: which words should I begin with?

It's one that business writers, particularly, struggle to answer. How seldom in the world of work do we read anything that draws us in and engages us right from the opening sentence? On the rare occasions that we do, it completely changes the way we think about the organisation whose voice we're hearing.

One of the great privileges of my working life is to sit on the board of the Edinburgh International Book Festival, the world's largest. I was glancing recently at last year's annual review and I came across this from our 2009 guest director, Richard Holloway, former Bishop of Edinburgh, now writer, broadcaster and commentator:

> *Annual reports tend to be jaunty affairs, celebrating past achievements, as the organisation in question strides confidently on into the future. Well, it wouldn't be dishonest to adopt that tone in reviewing my own wild fling … as guest director this year, but it would be the wrong way to begin, so I won't start there.*

For the business world, this is an unusually confident and personal piece of writing. But why should that be so? Why do chairmen's and chief executive's statements, not to mention letters, brochures and mail shots, so often sound robotic? Whatever the reason (and we'll be looking at this a few weeks down the line), their opening words set the tone for what follows and frequently leave us as readers struggling to stay interested.

Richard's opening does at least three things that guarantee we'll go with him. He pokes a little gentle fun at the genre, so we know at once that this is not going to be earnest (which is not to say it won't be serious); he introduces a lively voice — his own — which is not that of the organisation, but which we know speaks *for* the organisation; and he tempts us with a question: *why* doesn't he want to start with the jaunty view?

Personal though he sounds, this is still business writing in an important public document that reports on the affairs of our book festival to a very wide range of interested and influential people. Yet I'm sure that any one of those people who read the opening sentence would have felt compelled to read on.

116 THINGS TO DO

Take three examples of impersonal business writing. You can choose them from websites, or perhaps annual reports. Think of two people you know well — a friend or a member of your family. Now write the first example in the tone of voice of the first person you thought of — as if he or she were sitting talking to you. Do the same with the second, but think about how the tone of voice is different. Then write the third piece in your own tone of voice, as naturally as you can. Compare to the originals: how far would those organisations have allowed you to stretch? Perhaps further than you (or they) might have imagined.

Week 4
John to Jamie

CONSTRAINTS LIBERATE

We all feel the pressure to produce a piece of writing quickly — and to get it accepted quickly. *Time is of the essence.* But speed is not necessarily essential. You need to play a little more with your words, to make them better than just quickly produced and OK. Take a little time and reap the rewards.

I guess that's why we suggest the 'things to do' exercises. We're saying that writing is not an exact science — there can be any number of ways to write something, and perhaps the most obvious way is not the best. If that path ahead looks really well-trodden, it'll be heavy going. So, is there a more interesting path?

Constraints liberate: this sounds as if it should not be true. But I've discovered the truth of that counter-intuitive statement as I've gained more and more writing experience. In a previous book, *26 Ways of Looking at a Blackberry*, I probably tested its truth to the limit, rewriting a business text in 26 different ways. Some of the ways were technical shifts, such as eight-word sentences, a change of pronouns, writing without the vowel 'e' (hats off to Perec). Others took me into different forms of writing altogether: a fairy story, Shakespearean sonnet, song lyric, speech by Barack Obama and a graphic novel. The important point was not to find one form or one right answer, but to keep an open mind. There's always another way.

Constraints work. In the business world the commonest constraint is the brief. Is it a good brief? What is a good brief? Harry Pearce, a designer friend of mine who loves conundrums, said to me last week: 'Sometimes the more cornered you are, the more fun you have.' The result was a 'holiday season' (Christmas) catalogue for New York's Saks Fifth Avenue store that is, in a puzzling way, good to read as well as to shop from, and was based around conundrums.

We all need to find our own writing voice. We also need to find the voice of the company, organisation or brand we are writing for in the world of work. But we certainly owe it to ourselves to explore our own creativity fully. There are surprises if you open yourself up to that possibility and grasp it with enthusiasm. And writers who surprise themselves are more likely to surprise and entertain readers.

115 THINGS TO DO

That last document you wrote was OK, wasn't it?
Well, no one said it was rubbish — but no one said
they loved it. Take a couple of paragraphs and rewrite

them. First, rewrite them in the style of a novelist
you've read recently. Then rewrite the same words in
the style of your favourite writer of children's books.

Jamie to John

WRITING SANS FRONTIÈRES

There's another side to this constraints coin. Whenever I think
of it I see myself aged 23 on a large horse careering across a field
in Argentina.

There are several things about that image that still make me
shiver. One, I'm not a natural horseman: in fact horses frighten me
and this one knew it. Two, the ground was covered with termite
hills, three feet high, baked hard as concrete, and tapering to sharp
points. Three, fields in Argentina are the size of English counties.
Clinging to my steed's neck, I thought the ride would never end.

Sometimes, I get the same feeling when I have to write
something, particularly to the sort of brief that ends with the client
saying vaguely, 'Oh, you know the kind of thing we want...'

I go home, sit down and look at my notes and there's a horrible
moment of paralysis. It's not simply where do I start, but where on
earth do I *stop?* How am I going to give this thing structure, form,
some boundaries so that my thoughts don't just slither about like
amoebas and go wobbling over the edge of the earth?

So I look for whatever I can find that will help to contain
the job and make it seem manageable. There's always something.
Maybe it's the word count. Maybe it's the designer's layout. Maybe
it's something the client said that I hadn't picked up on. And
if none of those are available, I work through my notes to start
giving some kind of shape to what I *do* know. Perhaps there's a
chronological flow to the information or some kind of inherent
organisational logic. Perhaps there's an argument to be made or a
story to be told.

Whatever it is, I'm looking for a constraint, something that encloses the work I have to do and makes me feel safe in the knowledge that it *will* end and that I can get there; that I'm not back in that seemingly boundary-less Argentine field. Constraints don't just liberate, you see. They also protect you from the void, which we writers tend to know as the *blank page*.

114 THINGS TO DO

The report you have to write, the one you've been putting off because it seems so mountainous that all your energy drains away whenever you think about it... Try making a list of everything that will limit it and give it shape. Break it down into sections if necessary — going smaller makes things seem more manageable. Imagine yourself in a field that's small enough for you to see clearly all the fences and gates and other features. That should be your report.

Week 5
John to Jamie

OH, THE PLACES YOU'LL GO

The word 'liberate' brings us back to a writing project we're both involved in at the moment. As PEN International's Writers in Prison Committee is 50 years old this year, through the writers' group 26 we have set ourselves and other writers a formidable challenge. We've paired 50 writers from 26 with 50 writers nominated by PEN — one for each year 1960–2010. We've then asked each writer to produce exactly 50 words on the PEN writer as part of the ongoing campaign for freedom of expression. It sounds contradictory (such a restriction to champion the cause of freedom). But, as you say, the constraint protects you from the void — and it also takes you to an unusual place. I hadn't imagined that I would ever write about Indonesian dragons. Yet there I was, writing 50 words about Mochtar Lubis, a writer imprisoned several times for words that Indonesian dictators tried to suppress.

The beauty of this kind of project is that the tightness of the constraint takes you somewhere unexpected. You could argue, and some have, that the brief might have been to write no more than 50 words. Still tight, but a little bit more flexible than exactly 50 words. But I really think that it would not have worked nearly as well. I know from my own 50 words how I had to keep coming back to them, almost like one of those puzzles where you move little plastic squares inside a bigger square tray. New thoughts, better ideas, different words kept popping up as a result of trying to get to the exact 50.

As an editor of some of the other writers in the project I saw this happening with them, too. One writer sent me a beautiful piece (in two languages). But it was only 49 words. I asked for another word. The writer went back to her research and discovered that she'd slightly misquoted 'official' words in bureaucratic English. The real, and now revised, version was much more chilling and powerful in this context, and it magically brought the word count up to 50.

Another writer sent through a piece that was written in the form of a job ad — for an impossible job, carried out by one of the world's most famous political prisoners (Aung San Suu Kyi). It was only 48 words. The resolution was easy and brought about an improvement — I suggested the two words 'Apply within', and these provided the call to action that the ad had previously lacked.

The power of serendipity. It works, like the cat with the magical hat. You go to places you never thought you'd go. My daughter Jessie quoted these lines to me this week from Dr Seuss' *Oh, the Places You'll Go*:

Today is your day.
Your mountain is waiting.
So... get on your way.

113 THINGS TO DO

Write exactly 50 words about a writer whose work you
want to champion. Not 49, not 51, but exactly 50.
See what happens to your language as you do this,
as each word becomes precious. Write it by hand and
keep each draft you produce, so that when finished,
you can look back at the journey you undertook.

Mochtar Lubis, 1962
I imagine you
an Indonesian dragon:
your words the dragon's
teeth that sprang fully
armed from the writer's mouth.

Your dragon's eye
saw things your keepers
preferred to keep hidden.

They blinked first but
dragons don't blink:
you spat words, like
teeth, through prison bars.

The cage kept springing
open.

John Simmons

Xosé Luís Méndez Ferrín, 1972
You and the general
Shared a birthright
That awkward bastard
Mouthful of splinters
Your native tongue
But when he placed
His boot upon it

He forgot that hobnails
In the prison diet
Hone resistance
Whet contempt
While truth
Like blood or spittle
Finds its way
When even tongues are tied

Jamie Jauncey

Jamie to John

UNCHAINED

When I think of these imprisoned writers I picture damp, dingy cells and furtive scribblings on shreds of paper with pencil stubs, scrapings on prison walls with bent nails, even etchings with pins on crumbs of soap — all from minds desperate to find some way of expressing the precious ideas to which sanity and dignity are so closely linked. Yet such is the power of language that these extraordinary constraints often give rise to work of great power and even beauty, while helping safeguard their authors' souls from despair.

But language can also lie like a yoke across our backs, and we don't have to look far to see this. Take Edinburgh, where I do much of my work. Among the professions there, language remains utilitarian at best, anachronistic at worst. There are no high desks, wing collars or quill pens any longer but their traces linger in the Adam cornices, the panelling and picture frames of many a fine New Town building. They make their presence felt in some of the more fustian turns of phrase — 'upon receipt of' for example — still liable to grace an accountant's report or a lawyer's letter.

Last summer I ran a workshop for one of those august institutions, a professional body. I was there because they recognised the need to bring their language into the 21st century, particularly at the point of contact with their 20,000 plus members; although since they are also the regulator for their profession, the poor folk in the membership team lead a schizophrenic existence, wearing customer service smiles one moment and traffic warden frowns the next.

But the will to change was there. My small group worked hard to dust away the cobwebs, cast off the shackles of a century or more of institution-speak. 'Members are people too', said one of the group at one point, and I raised a silent cheer.

Once the workshop was over, I walked along to the Edinburgh International Book Festival. Here, in the magical tented village that springs up every August, there was not a linguistic shackle in sight. On the contrary, language in Charlotte Square is celebrated. It takes flight. It moves, inspires, tickles, infuriates, terrifies, thrills. It flows through the marquees like the life force itself and everywhere you look people are immersed in it, up to their necks in words, up to their eyes in stories, up to the crowns of their heads in ideas.

A mere half-mile apart, here were two groups of people, the one effectively imprisoned by language, the other entirely liberated by it. And, not for the first time, I found myself wondering whether perhaps it suits the world of business to continue using language as a ball and chain. Because the alternative — people who are literally empowered and liberated by language — seems too alarming and unpredictable.

112 THINGS TO DO

Who is your favourite writer? Dip into their work again. Think hard about what they do that you like so much. Is it the way they tell a story? Is it the kind of words or phrases they use? What is it that brings their writing to life, gives it energy and makes you want to read on? Make a list. Then take something you have to write at work and try it as if you were your favourite author.

John to Jamie

THE WORD LESS CHOSEN

I like the unexpected word in your last piece — *fustian*. It's not a word that we use a lot but it conjures up images of pompous professionals, dark-suited in dark offices. Individual words, particularly unexpected ones, have this power to create pictures; and they're also containers of our attitudes. Often, companies steer away from words that make pictures but, without intending to, they manage to convey, through their vocabulary, sometimes contempt, sometimes hostility to their audiences.

Words also make connections, which reminds me that 'only connect' is my favourite quotation. It comes from EM Forster's *Howards End*. It came to my mind again this week when we were speakers at a 'narrative conference for the Welsh public service' in Llandudno. As we walked to the conference centre along the windswept seafront, it seemed an attractive prospect to take refuge in storytelling.

In these deficit days, I remain a believer in the value of public service. But sometimes I despair at the failure of language used to make the case for it. At the conference I enjoyed the first speaker, Geoff Mead, a policeman turned academic. His focus was on leadership and the role of storytelling (actually 'narrative' as the academic world generally prefers the more erudite choice of word). He said many interesting things, among them his preference for using the active verb 'leading' rather than the inert noun 'leadership'. So we were on the same wavelength. He talked, too, about the difference between story and factual argument, between 'mythos' and 'logos'. This seemed to set things in the right direction.

Through the afternoon, you, Stuart Delves and I ran workshops. I concentrated on mythology, the most fundamental form of storytelling. First I got people to discuss those words — generally abstract nouns — that are the formulaic words in the communication of their own sector. Having flushed them out, the words were ready to be explored, given new meaning and perhaps even laughed out of existence through the creation of myths about them.

The words and phrases were: *sustainability, performance improvement, social inclusion, content management, evaluation, equality, change programme, participation, standards, accessibility, knowledge management, partnership.* The dirty dozen words of public sector management. Or perhaps not confined only to the public sector? We all recognise and shudder at many of those phrases.

Why? Because they are empty vessels. Intended to convey vast amounts of meaning in shorthand form, they do very little except tick boxes on evaluation forms. So people explored what they really meant — through their own storytelling. And in the words of one participant: 'You made a roomful of civil servants manic'. Were we doing a public service? Probably.

I'm not trying to ban these or other words. Many of them are unlikely candidates for classification as jargon. But I find it sad that language gets devalued through lazy and often bureaucratic use, ending up as management-speak. I feel for good words like 'partnership' and 'participation'. It seems they have been suffering from abuse. We should restore them — and others like them — to a healthier life full of meaning. Stories help us to discover and reveal that meaning.

111 THINGS TO DO

What are the buzzwords of your business world? Customer experience? Leverage? Value? Choose one. What does it really mean? Discover its fuller meaning by writing a myth about it. Who is the god of that word? What does he/she do, and how do they do it? Let the story flow, have fun. You may be surprised at some new insights revealed.

ONLY CONNECT

Ah yes, Llandudno. With its guest houses and sedate hotels, its broad sweep of promenade and slightly incongruous palm trees, it's a place of stories if ever there was one: stories of holidays that went right, or wrong, or perhaps never happened at all, stories of local lives lived out to the sound of the waves rolling in from the bay. And every single one of them to do with human connections — made or missed, muddled or unmade.

Stories come in many guises and we can use them all at work, just as we do in life (now isn't *that* a telling distinction — we say there's *work* and then there's *life*…). Anyway, while you were at one end of the storytelling spectrum, taking big ideas and turning them into myths, I was right at the other end, encouraging my group to tell each other personal anecdotes.

In pairs, they had a few minutes each to recount to one another significant moments in their lives — turning points you might say. Then each listener re-told the story they had heard, in their own words, to the whole group. At the end of the re-telling they identified two personal characteristics, or values, that the story revealed, usually without the original teller realising it.

These were tales of personal triumphs or disasters, great or small, and everyone listened intently as each new tale unfolded. There were several things I wanted people to understand: firstly that stories, as the Nigerian novelist Ben Okri said, 'are the secret reservoirs of value', and that it's not only people that have them to tell: organisations do, too.

Secondly, it can be surprising, even illuminating, to hear your own story retold by someone else. This is because we always add something of our own to any story we tell, and that something might just be a fresh insight.

Lastly, and most importantly, I wanted people to experience how stories from ordinary lives can connect a roomful of strangers in a way that nothing else can; and how the real lightning conductor is language.

As you know so well, John, one just can't tell stories using words or phrases like 'sustainability', 'performance improvement', 'social inclusion' and 'content management'. Stories like the ones we heard in Llandudno can only be told in the words of daily conversation, which are rich in emotion and imagery. This is the only possible language for storytelling — and the only possible language of true human connection, at work or anywhere else.

110 THINGS TO DO

Founding stories particularly can be good 'reservoirs' of value. If your organisation's founding story has been consigned to the attic of corporate history, it might be worth getting it out and dusting it down to see what it tells you. What did your founders really stand for? What was their original vision for the organisation they were creating? What struggles did they go through to achieve it? Try re-telling that story for now and see if it refreshes your thoughts about what your organisation is doing and where it is going. See if it helps reconnect you and your colleagues with your sense of purpose and each other.

Week 7
John to Jamie

SHOUTS AND WHISPERS

There's great comfort in the words: 'Once upon a time…' We settle down before a metaphorical fireplace, ready to be drawn into the quiet telling of a story. But few pieces of writing now start like that. We know we have to grab people's attention, and we worry we might not have much time, so there's a temptation to start shouting. AMAZING OFFER!! So amazing it needs capitals and two exclamation marks.

Let's slow down, let's take a deep breath. For the series of two-day workshops I've been running for Orange, the mobile phone company, we always have an invited poet to read and talk. The other week it was Joe Dunthorne, a brilliant young poet. He talked about how he starts writing: 'Sometimes you start because you're inspired to write. But often it just takes a random phrase, something taken from a street sign or a book.' It works in the business world, too, because you find an unusual starting point. The phrase strikes a spark in your imagination. You then develop it and take it to a conclusion. The beginning, middle and end of storytelling.

This week I also went off to the V&A Museum in London. Working with a writer called Rob Self-Pierson, we're developing an idea for another 26 project ('26 Treasures'). Using the constraint of 'write exactly 62 words', I wrote about a Renaissance era statue of the Angel Gabriel. We put this poem in the proposal to the V&A.

He cleared his throat. And raised his fingers high.
The brass had seemed, well, just a little bit
Too crass. Big news can come without trumpets,
Be spoken quietly. No need for drama.

He'd folded wings, not wishing to cause flight.
Why not just take some time to think it through?
The angel stepped forward and spoke to us
All about expectations.

I liked the idea of Gabriel announcing big news so calmly. Has anyone in history or fiction ever had such a profound announcement to make?

Inevitably I thought about the writing that's all around us in the commercial world. As you walk down the street you see 'Fantastic Deals' everywhere. The internet has the same problem. In a web writing workshop for The Writer (www.thewriter.co.uk) I used this slide:

The most unbeatably effective way of making sure not one single reader ever reads your fantastic web writing is to fill it full of amazing adjectives and awesomely annoying 'salesy' waffle.

It's true. The next time you're tempted to use a string of superlatives to sell a new product or service, think again. There is another, better way. Think of the Angel Gabriel.

109 THINGS TO DO

So you have a sales message to write and your imagination is completely empty, but you know you want to avoid the shouting approach. Take a walk, look around, use your notebook to jot down phrases that interest you. When you come back, try a piece of automatic writing: 10 minutes non-stop, stream of consciousness, just starting with that phrase. Then immediately start to edit, thinking about your sales message. It will come out in a completely different way. Amazing!

Jamie to John

'THE TRAIN NOW ARRIVING...'

From The Annunciation to announcements. It's a short step in literal meaning but a giant one in practical reality, and never more so than when the announcements are of the public service variety. There's no better place to observe the phenomenon than on the railway (and no one knows it better then you, John. Didn't you once spend a week travelling the country to study a rail company's tone of voice?).

Anyway, put a man or woman in a train company uniform, hand them a microphone, and strange and terrible things start to happen. Vestibules appear. Passengers are advised that, 'This train is approaching Auchenshuggle, where the train will terminate'. Luggage is to be kept clear of the aisles AT ALL TIMES.

An hour on most trains is an hour in a linguistically barren world of a kind Orwell himself might have imagined when creating Newspeak, shot through with odd moments of Douglas Adams-esque lunacy. Essentially it's about control. Do this. Don't do that. On the better services passengers may be 'requested' to cooperate in some way. But the language remains authoritarian and the sub-text to most of it is: 'Now we've told you, so you can't blame us if something nasty happens.'

Very occasionally, however, a note of ordinary humanity slips through. This happened a couple of days ago when my train came to a sudden halt in the middle of the countryside. It was one of those uncharacteristically mild February days when you think that spring might have come early. After a wait of several minutes a cheery guard apologised on the tannoy for the delay, explaining that it was caused by children playing on the line. ('Of course they are,' said the elderly woman sitting opposite me, 'they've been cooped up inside all winter.')

The guard's tone was natural, conversational even. He was explaining to us what had happened as he might have done to his friends in the pub, later on that evening. I looked around. Most people were simply shrugging, one or two even smiling wryly. There were few brows furrowed in irritation or frustration.

Twenty minutes later we stopped at a big station and a different voice came over the loudspeaker system, apologising for the delay to passengers who had just boarded and explaining that it had been caused by 'trespassers on railway property'. Twenty minutes, I thought. That's how long it takes for railway-speak to reassert its authority. That's how long it takes for children to become trespassers.

108 THINGS TO DO

Next time you make a train journey, note down all the announcements you hear. Then try rewriting them as if this was an opportunity to really make contact with the passengers as human beings, as people who might be persuaded by your tone of voice that you wanted them to enjoy, and repeat, the experience of travelling on your trains.

IS THAT YOU CALLING ME?

You're right, I did once travel by train all around East Anglia when I was working on the tone of voice of announcements for Anglia Railways. Many years before that I'd worked with InterCity railways whose boss, John Prideaux, started speeches with the words, 'I love trains'. Now I'm no longer sure if he wrote that or if I did.

The retreat to the language of authority is common. Corporations love it, with or without the wearing of a uniform. And it's not just the 'public utilities' that take to it all too easily. I find it striking that even in the newest and biggest of global companies, you can hear a similar kind of bureaucratic tone — often in situations where they should be turning their friendliest and most human face to the world.

Take this example from Microsoft. They recently put out a press release with this headline:

> *Windows Phone 7. A Fresh Start for Smartphone. The Phone Delivers a New User Experience by Integrating the Things Users Really Want to Do, Creating a Balance Between Getting Work Done and Having Fun.*

Suddenly, railway announcements seem quite light and to the point. The initial capitals are Microsoft's in that example, not mine, and that's a very American convention that I find quite alienating. It's not just the words — though they're off-putting enough — it's the way the words look. Rather than an inviting headline — supposedly about 'having fun' — it comes across like one of those official notices forbidding you to trespass. And why do they believe a *headline* should be 34 words long?

When you go beyond the headline, it gets no better. This is how it continues:

The goal for Microsoft's latest smartphone is an ambitious one: to deliver a phone that truly integrates the things people really want to do, puts those things right in front of them, and either lets them get finished quickly or immerses them in the experience they were seeking.

I don't know about you, but my response to this is '?'. When you really work hard at it, translating it in effect, you reach some kind of understanding. But they are claiming that this phone will make your life easier. Shouldn't that start with the language they use to describe it?

Contrast that with Apple. When Steve Jobs introduced the iPhone in 2007, he said:

Today Apple is going to reinvent the phone. And here it is.

I know which one speaks to me.

107 THINGS TO DO

What's the story of your life so far? So much to tell, and where to start? Write it as a text message and see how much you can actually say before the box is full. Send it by phone to someone you know well and ask for their comments.

LOST IN TRANSLATION

You talk of having to 'translate' Microsoft's words. Anything that needs translating is lousy communication because it has lost any of the immediacy, and probably much of the power, it might once have had. And why should we bother, anyway? We didn't ask Microsoft to speak to us. So we move smartly on and Microsoft has missed an opportunity. If we really do have to know what they're saying, we trudge forward resentfully with furrowed brow.

Which brings me back again to your 'dirty dozen' — *sustainability, performance improvement, social inclusion,* etc. The problem for these perfectly valid words is that being lazy, the organisational world makes them work far harder than they were ever intended to. It makes them stand there naked, alone and in not-so-splendid abstraction, rather like the first Martians on earth, sole representatives of something huge, unseen and often very complex.

Abstractions are the bane of working life. They're everywhere, a shorthand for everything, and they use none of the currency of normal human exchange — concrete ideas, emotions, metaphors, tangible images of people doing things. Try wringing an image or a feeling from *sustainability.* It simply doesn't work. So you're left with something whose real meaning, if you can be bothered at all, you have to delve for.

Microsoft's press release falls into this trap. It might sound good but it veers towards abstraction and tells you practically nothing. '… a phone that truly integrates the things people really want to do,' and 'immerses them in the experience they were seeking'. Do those two statements leave any pictures in your mind?

A theme I know we're both going to return to time and again in this book is the need for emotion in good communication. This doesn't mean that everything we write should bring a tear to the reader's eye, but it does mean that good writing at work, as anywhere else, should have energy, colour, warmth, personality, conviction — all the ingredients, in fact, which can never be present in abstractions such as *performance improvement*. Even the two simple words 'doing better' convey more feeling than that.

The children's novelist, Philip Pullman, was leading a group of writers to protest at publishers' plans to badge children's books according to the age band for which they were deemed appropriate (the plan happily fizzled out). At a meeting with senior publishing industry figures, he opened with an impassioned warning of the perils of attempting to homogenise readership.

The leading publisher heard him out, then requested that they keep the emotion out of the discussion and consider things rationally — to which, so the story goes, Philip Pullman responded that he would very much prefer to keep the emotion *in*, if they didn't mind, since this was an issue about which a great many people felt very strongly.

You don't even need to feel that strongly about something to justify keeping the emotion in. It's simply the basis of all good communication.

106 THINGS TO DO

Take one of those all-purpose business words like 'sustainability' or 'innovation' (two real corkers, and there are loads of others) and make a list of all the things they could possibly mean without using further abstractions. In other words, you should describe them in terms of real people doing real things — so that they create images in your mind.

Week 9
John to Jamie

IS THAT A METAPHOR I SEE BEFORE ME?

One way, perhaps the best way, of retaining the emotion is to use metaphors. That's why we've called this book *Room 121* rather than, say, *Business Writing One-to-One*. However shadowy the picture might be, a reader can see a door with a number on it and imagine going through that door to find...what?

The imagination kicks in. You find that you've engaged better with your reader because you've planted an image in their mind. When we run workshops together, we know that an exercise about the creation of metaphors is going to transform the way people think and write.

There are times — it happens with all writers — when you feel stuck. Your words are dry, there's no real feeling in them. Then, often magically (but practice helps), a metaphor can come riding to the rescue. There you are, stuck in the middle of a desert, not a thought in sight, no idea within reach. But then the metaphor appears in front of you, not just vivid and real but capable of changing the landscape of what you write. Inspired by the metaphor, you start adding details that bring your writing to life. The argument becomes clearer, no longer a mirage but a real oasis.

A metaphor is a vivid picture. It also reinforces for me that I enjoy working with designers. When you're writing words while thinking how a designer might respond to them, it affects the way you write. Words and images are a creative resource, and they work well together.

Are these separate ways of thinking? I'd say they are complementary. In my experience there's no big divide between writers and designers. The good designers that I know are all good with words — they appreciate working with writers who add something visual to their work. Words can provide that extra creative spark, particularly if the writer also thinks visually.

105 THINGS TO DO

Think of a close friend, someone you know well. When you're thinking of that friend, what season comes into your mind? What natural things do you associate with that season? Now write a line to describe your friend while referring to that particular season.

OF SOUP AND SEA

One of the most striking metaphors I've heard recently was offered by Noel Gallagher, from the band Oasis, speaking of his brother Liam. The two have been at war since adolescence. 'Liam,' said Noel wearily, 'is a man with a fork in a world of soup.'

It's such a vivid and lasting image of someone at odds with himself and everyone around him. Ten simple words that conjure a whole life — both funny and tragic at the same time.

Metaphors work because they bring the commonplace to life in fresh and unexpected ways. Take a rather dull example — insurance. Even such an obvious metaphor as the safety net strung below the high-wire artist in the roof of the big top goes some way to energising a thoroughly over-familiar idea, and leaves one with a lasting mental image.

Metaphors can work in much more profound ways, too. The exercises you refer to, John, the ones we run in our courses, can quickly bring people to tears through their sheer power to reconnect us with things and other people we take for granted.

They can also help us to take a fresh look at problems. An exercise I sometimes do to illustrate this is to ask people to come up with a metaphor for an issue or topic they're dealing with at work. Then, working with a partner, and restricting themselves to the world of that particular metaphor, they extend the story it tells, and interrogate it.

In a recent group, one person who was fairly new to the organisation came up with the well-worn image of being out of her depth. But, with helpful questions from the person she was paired with, she was able to look more closely at the story she was telling and came to see that she was in the relatively safe waters of a calm bay, that she was swimming strongly and keeping her head above water, and that there were plenty of people within shouting distance on the beach, who were keeping an eye out for her.

By the same token, metaphor can be a powerful tool for examining the health of an organisation. One group I worked with came up with the memorable metaphor of orangutan King Louie's hideout, from the movie of *The Jungle Book* — a ruined, creeper-ridden palace swarming with out-of-control monkeys — for their recently-merged financial institution.

We use metaphor all the time, so much so that we usually don't even notice it. Yet somehow, that naturally playful, imaginative faculty so often gets left at the office door. We'd all be better communicators if we remembered to bring it in with us.

104 THINGS TO DO

Can you find a good metaphor for what your business or organisation does? One that hasn't been used before? Once you've got one, see if you can extend it to make room for what you yourself do there, so your job becomes part of the metaphor too. Next time someone asks you about your work, try describing it this way.

Week 10
John to Jamie

REMEMBER POETRY

I'm picking up on a word in your last sentence, Jamie, because 'remember' goes to the heart of the power of metaphor and poetry, particularly in the world of business writing.

Most businesses want you to remember them and to pick them out when faced with a choice. So, writing words that are easily remembered — and associated with a particular company, brand or product — is an important objective for a writer, especially for an advertising copywriter.

This was brought home again by the latest McDonald's ad on TV. This has the actor David Morrissey speaking the words in his light Liverpudlian accent. It grabbed my attention the first time I heard it and I keep enjoying it. My first thought was that it was a poem by Roger McGough. Later I discovered that it was actually written by copywriters at the ad agency Leo Burnett, who had based it on the lyrics of a song by Rolf Harris. Strange but true. In part it goes....

the Gothy types and scoffy types
and like-their-coffee-frothy types
were just passing by

It's unusual — and memorable — to come across a TV ad that takes such obvious enjoyment in playing with words: words that are poetry. Poetry is not used that often in business writing but when it is, it can be very effective. Poetic techniques have passed down the centuries because they recognise the need for memorability. Rhyme, alliteration and repetition are an aid to the listener, the reader or the storyteller, encouraging them to remember the words.

Whenever I hear the words 'I remember' my brain is triggered to recite in my head the words from Thomas Hood's poem that I remember from my childhood:

I remember, I remember
The house where I was born.

I've enjoyed using poetic techniques when writing for businesses. Coleridge's lines from his long poem *Kubla Khan* came into my head when, many years ago, I was working on a new brand of goat's cheese. And 'for he on honey-dew hath fed/and drunk the milk of paradise' appeared on the packaging.

This morning I was pushing a shopping trolley around Marks & Spencer. Ten years ago I wrote many of the M&S words that appeared on packaging, point of sale and shop signs. Most of it has now gone, inevitably replaced over time. But one example at least remains, staring at me from the sign on the shopping trolley: 'Too heavy? Too far? Collect by car.'

So you haven't written much poetry? Perhaps not since you were at school? Try writing a *haiku* — it's a very short poem, Japanese in origin, made up of just three lines. The important thing is the number of syllables in each line; 5 in the first, 7 in the second, 5 in the third, with no need to rhyme. Use the *haiku* to give yourself some advice about writing. Be strict with yourself about keeping to the exact number of syllables.

Post finished haikus
on your computer as a
daily reminder.

Jamie to John

VERSE AND WORSE

Here's a poem I wrote a few years ago when a financial services client appointed a number of people as communications champions and sent them forth throughout the organisation to do — well, no one was quite sure what. I thought the poem might help shed a little light on the matter, but the client didn't really understand it and I think it ended up in her 'things I'm not sure what to do with' file. I had fun writing it, though.

So — you've a new breed
Of warrior poets
Primed to bear witness
The breadth of the land
Bards for our time
Tellers of stories
These are the knights
Who will champion your brand

Oh — they'll need more
Than plain understanding
To rally their fellows
Strike fire in their breasts
They must seek language
That sparks and ignites
They must choose words
The brightest and best

Where will they find them
These glistening objects
Vibrant with meaning
Polished and true?
By looking within
To what their hearts tell them
That's where the light
Of conviction shines through

They must relinquish
Their corporate armour
Dare to be human
That's how they'll engage
Unshackle their passion
Their imagination
And find a new voice
To resound in our age

Of course, you don't even need to resort to verse or rhyme to bring a little poetry to what you write. We both begin workshops with a simple but illuminating exercise that I think you devised years ago, John. We ask everyone present to name a favourite word. The resulting list allows us to make the point that we all have a relationship with words that goes well beyond their simple meaning.

Recently, for example, 'onomatopoeia' and 'hippopotamus' were two of the words offered on a workshop I was running. Why did you choose that word, I asked the participants? Because of the way it sounds, answered one. Because of the rhythm, said the other.

In the meaning-obsessed world of business, we tend to exclude the 'non-essential' qualities of language. Our writer's palettes remain a dreary monochrome, our voices a dull monotone. And if some kind of pulse or poetry does creep in, it's less likely to be for purposes of enlivening the writing, more likely to be out of fear that if we don't say the same thing three times, people will think we've only done a third of the job.

'Design, develop and implement' is a favourite, beloved of that great droning swarm of strategificators and initiative-creators who populate all modern organisations. But as poetry goes, that string of three verbs has all the charm and subtlety of a hammer hitting a thumb. As for meaning, why in God's name would you design something if you didn't intend to develop and implement it? What happened to good old-fashioned planning, anyway?

As you so rightly said, John, it all goes back to making what you write memorable. Poetry, and what's naturally poetic in language, helps. 'Design, develop and implement' doesn't.

102 THINGS TO DO

What are your favourite words? Not the obvious ones that we now ban from workshops — like 'Friday', 'weekend', 'holiday', 'sunshine', 'chocolate' — but those words that have stuck inside your head for no other reason than that you like them. Next time you have to write something, see if you can work one or two of them into your text.

Week 11
John to Jamie

THE END OF SHAKESPEARE

We know people are intimidated by poetry — we see it often in workshops. But if there's a fear of poetry, there's probably an even greater fear of Shakespeare. For too many people he's a writer who arouses resentment because of unhappy school encounters. People have bad memories of having to 'do Shakespeare'. There's no other writer you have to 'do' in quite the same way.

Much of this fear comes from misunderstanding. You don't have to revere every word Shakespeare wrote. He was a pragmatic, collaborative writer. I suspect he was far more willing to see his words changed in the mouths of others — fellow actors — than some presentday copywriters who insist their work cannot be changed. We all have clients, as did Shakespeare. Sometimes his clients were Queen Elizabeth and King James, rather than those we might be working for, such as a marketing manager in a supermarket chain. Perhaps Shakespeare's clients had more clout. I'm sure he was keen to please them so he thought hard about how to apply his craft.

A few years ago, we both took part in writing a 26 project called 'The Bard & Co'. In this book we wrote about the relevance of Shakespeare to modern business writers. I became particularly interested in the very formal constraint of a sonnet, and now we regularly use sonnets as an exercise on our Dark Angels courses.

The sonnets tell us much about rhythm, alliteration, metaphor, choice of words. There is also something important in the sonnet's formal journey from beginning to middle to end. Perhaps, Jamie, that's just a simpler version of 'design, develop and implement'? Within a few lines (just 14) a sonnet demonstrates how to develop a thought or feeling into an argument, and then to bring everything to a satisfying ending.

In our workshops we focus particularly on the two lines that close a sonnet, the couplet. People worry about creating their own versions of couplets, something they're not used to doing in conventional business writing. They spend time thinking not just about choosing the right words to express the meaning, but also listening hard to the sound of words. They listen to language, and they listen to the way a couplet sends a clear signal of completeness.

You probably won't have to write a sonnet at work, but I would argue that we need to do something very similar when writing for business. When it comes to endings, we need to listen and judge whether we have closed our argument as satisfyingly as a Shakespearean couplet. It's like those stories of car-makers being obsessive about the sound of a closing car door.

You know it makes sense.
Think differently.
Just do it.
Believe.

101 THINGS TO DO
Think of your favourite end-line in an advert. Google it and you'll find lists of other lines. Listen to them. Which ones are real endings, like the car door closing? Improve those that you think need improving.

Jamie to John

SPIT AND POLISH

You've mentioned two poetic forms in the last couple of weeks — *haiku* and sonnets. Both set challenging constraints. Both demand that you think very hard about what you have to say, choosing your words carefully. It's most unlikely that you'll complete either a sonnet or a haiku at the first pass. The sonnet will have an untidy thought that needs polishing, the haiku a word that needs changing to set the syllable count right.

The first draft of anything is seldom the best. If you want your writing to hit the mark and be memorable, you owe it to yourself not to press 'send' as soon as you reach the final full stop. Even a trip to the coffee machine or a walk down the corridor can be enough to subtly alter your perception of what you've just written when you return. An absence of only a couple of minutes can put the spotlight on that little passage of woolly thinking or throw that awkward phrase into relief. And you'll notice even more if you've been able to leave it overnight.

I've always thought of editing as almost the most creative part of the whole process. The second draft of my novels is when I've told the story and got to the end, and now I can polish and fine tune, sculpt, tweak and fiddle. I'm free of the pressure to keep the narrative moving along. Oddly enough, it is the stage at which I feel I'm really giving full rein to my craft, and it's actually the most satisfying part of the process.

Working with a sympathetic editor who's in tune with the story and characters is more satisfying still. When you've written, say, 80,000 words, no matter how punctilious you are, the law of averages is against you and some of them are going to be wrong. A good editor will pick up the things you simply can't see; the relationship becomes a collaboration whose goal is to turn the book into a better one than you could have written on your own.

At work, of course, we tend not to have editors, but we do have colleagues who can read what we've written and spot the things we miss. And if the pressures of business life mean that you won't have the luxury of several weeks' polishing time, or even several days, just a few minutes can still make the difference between something that merely does the job and something that has a little shine to it.

100 THINGS TO DO

Sit down for just five minutes with the most recent thing you've written. Where could you improve it, give it more substance, make it more memorable, or even just more succinct and to the point? Rewrite it then show it to a colleague.

Week 12

John to Jamie

ASK THE EDITOR

The overnight rule is a good one. I wish I could say I always adopt it. But, as you say, we're all under time pressure.

Even so, it's vital to give time to editing. The word can mean many things to many people but this quotation from a poet, Billy Collins, helps to define what we're talking about:

> *I'll write a couple of lines, a sentence or a stanza, and I'll stop and say: 'Okay, I just wrote that but how would a stranger read it?' If someone were just picking this up, does it make any sense? Does it have any charm? Does it have any momentum? And then I go back to being a writer. I do this quite intuitively: writer-reader-writer-reader-writer...*

I find this interesting and wonder if the role of the 'reader' is different from that of the 'editor'. In the business world, editor is the term we're more used to. But I wonder if neither model is correct; we need to see this not as a dialogue but as a three-sided conversation. Perhaps it should really be 'writer-reader-editor-writer-reader-editor'. With each model, it's vital for the writer to take responsibility for the other roles, too. Be your own reader, be your own editor.

So there is an essential act, perhaps more readily associated with the fiction writer than the business writer, to step outside what you have written and imagine its effect on your reader. I've recently been writing words to go on the packaging of Pronamel toothpaste. There was a tight restriction in terms of number of words, so editing was needed in a technical sense just to get down to the right word count. But I also found it important to understand and imagine the situation of a consumer who might be persuaded to buy this toothpaste rather than one of the other brands.

When you're editing, you need to edit with a strong sense of who your reader might be. Ask yourself questions to build a better picture of that reader in your mind. Even if you'll have thousands of readers, it will only be read by one person at a time. So write, read and edit, imagining how your reader might respond to your words.

Jamie to John

FACING BACKWARDS

When I'm talking to people about 'being the reader' I always literally take that step you describe and move through 180 degrees, so that I'm facing the place where I was standing before. It's a physical illustration of how we must be able to assume both roles in order to write well. What it really comes down to, of course, is empathy — which in turn depends on imagination.

To drive the point home I argue that most acts of brutality are failures, or deliberate suspensions, of imagination: if the perpetrators were able, or allowed themselves, to empathise with their victims they would never commit the acts.

Happily, lack of empathy in writing doesn't often lead to acts of brutality. If it does, they're likely to be against inanimate objects — the document in question, for example. But it does very often result in a real failure of connection, even a sense of alienation.

Just before Christmas I went to see Richard Wright's Turner Prize-winning creation at Tate Britain. A vast gold-leaf fresco of mesmerising power and beauty, 'creation' seems the right word for it because that is just what it conjured for me: the Creation.

Minutely detailed shapes seethed, swirled and flowed in a gorgeous torrent of gold across a huge expanse of white wall. It had an almost religious intensity, like something by Blake or Michelangelo. I could have gazed at it for hours.

Then I looked at the programme. Here is one sentence: 'Wright accepts and virtually reverses the effects of attrition, re-assessing correlative notions of value and preservation, a virtue running across his practice.'

I pushed the programme crossly back in my pocket and thought, here is a double failure of empathy. Not only was it written in the absurd, pretentious, scarcely intelligible language of art-speak, but also it told me only what the curator wanted to say, which in almost no way coincided with what I experienced or wanted to know.

We come across this so often in business writing. The organisation trumpets what it wants to say with barely a thought for what the reader wants to know; when a moment's reflection, a moment of making that 180 degree movement, would result in a real connection with the reader, rather than a sense of distance and annoyance.

And what are the things I would really have liked to have been told about Richard Wright? Firstly, that he's steeped in the history of art and draws on influences as old as they are broad. Secondly, that he never knows what he will create until he steps into the space where he's going to exhibit. Thirdly, that his work is impermanent; he paints it straight onto the wall and paints over it when the show ends.

98 THINGS TO DO

How would you feel if you had to read your own work? Would you really want to read it? Take a recent e-mail, report or anything else you've had to write, and make the conscious effort to read it as if you were the person, or one of the people, you wrote it for. It might help to go and sit somewhere different while you do it. What would you change?

THE BUSINESS OF ART, THE ART OF BUSINESS

Some readers might be thinking: what's all this talk of art? Poetry, paintings, performances? Museums and galleries? What has this got to do with business?

The question might have been a legitimate one a couple of decades ago but now the 'creative industries' are big business. The latest government figures tell us that the creative industries are more important to the economy than financial services. Businesses, and countries, now need to succeed by the power of their imaginations rather than by their ability to trade hardware. So we'll continue to mix in references to our work with arts organisations alongside our work with banks and insurance companies.

The '26 Treasures' project is now developing well with the V&A (see *Week 7*). The Museum has agreed to be partners with our writing group 26 on this project, which explores the inspiration provided by objects. The curator of the British Galleries at the V&A will choose 26 objects; then we'll ask 26 writers to respond to those objects in a personal way, using exactly 62 words. The results will be revealed in the autumn as part of the London Design Festival.

The idea started with Rob Self-Pierson's suggestion, 'Let's see if the National Gallery might be interested in us writing about 26 of their paintings'. The idea then moved towards the V&A. Our original, and continuing, determination is to write about art and precious objects in a way that avoids the deadening language of art-speak. Effectively what people will do is get to know their object — in my case, an 18th century Rococo candle stand — through research and observation. But also (as you just wrote) through empathy. We'll need to show empathy with the object itself ('What kind of life have you led, candle stand?') and also with the visitors to the V&A. How can we help visitors feel a connection between the object and their own lives and emotions?

It seems clear to me that this is the way you have to write about art — by showing empathy and emotion. Art isn't an academic exercise, and even academic writing needs to express the emotions aroused by art. Otherwise we might as well be describing a new house contents policy (but are the two really that different?).

It all reminds me that a couple of years ago I worked on presenting the identity of the National Gallery. The design consultancy, The Partners, decided to use words rather than a visual symbol that obviously could not possibly compete with the Da Vincis, Goyas and Picassos inside the gallery. So I came up with a list of 50 words that expressed the states of mind depicted by, and aroused by, great art. Adverts appeared listing 'devotion', 'ecstasy' and 'revenge', for example, but the list always ended with the words: 'LIFE DEATH PASSION BEAUTY'.

In effect we were saying that all human life, all its emotions, are here. Could an insurance company not say it was dealing with the same emotions? Should it not reflect that fact more creatively in its use of language?

97 THINGS TO DO

Imagine that you're taking out a new insurance policy on the contents of your house. Start making a list of items to be covered, beginning with the ones that are most precious to you personally, but not necessarily the most valuable in money terms. Take one of those objects and write about it, as quickly as you can, perhaps from the point of view of that object. What 'experiences' has it witnessed?

THE REAL MCCOY

Of course an insurance company should use more creative language. In fact, why would it ever *not* want to? Although I must admit that I find myself becoming increasingly wary of that word 'creatively'. I think it's widely misunderstood in the business world and it can come to represent a pressure to go in a direction that many people find unfathomable and alarming.

The word is often used in workshops I'm running. 'We know our subject but we want to be able to write about it a bit more creatively,' people say. And I can see in their eyes that the thought carries with it the suggestion, if not of the novelist's or screenwriter's studio, at least of the copywriting department of an advertising agency — a glamorous, high-octane world populated by ironic 30-somethings with interesting haircuts and sackfuls of bright ideas.

But for anyone who doesn't fit that description — which is most people — it's an unrealistic and quite unnecessary aspiration. You see, I'm coming more and more to the conclusion that creativity, in absolutely any context you care to name, means something a lot more basic and universal. It means, quite simply, being yourself. In fact, I'd almost prefer to substitute the word 'authenticity'. (And to all those businesses that say, 'We need to value creativity more highly' — a concept they only vaguely understand anyway — I'd reply: 'No you don't. You need to value authenticity more highly. Let the world know who you really are and what you really stand for. And if you don't know, it's high time you found out.')

So what does authenticity mean when you have to write that pensions brochure? The selfsame thing. It means knowing who you are and writing about it in a way that sounds and feels natural to you, the writer; your own way, in fact, the way you would talk about it to a friend (another intelligent, literate adult, just like you). It means acknowledging that a pension is not a sports car or a cruise, but that it is something that may one day become incredibly important to the reader, whose retirement it will guarantee.

The opposite of 'authentic' is 'fake'. If you read a novel that sounds fake, you say it's a bad novel. In the business world we put up with writing that sounds fake all the time, and we know it. But if we read something that rings true, that has personality, some basic human warmth — that sounds authentic, in fact — do we say it's creative? Probably not. But that is undoubtedly what it is.

96 THINGS TO DO

We take so many things for granted — the fakeness of much of what we read in business, for example. It's just there, and it's too much effort to do anything about. But what about examining our own ignorance? Those words whose meaning you're never totally sure about, those sayings that have a point but you've never been able to figure out what exactly. Get into the habit of looking things up — it's never been easier, after all. Start with the title of this post. Who was the real McCoy?

Part 2

SPRING

Week 14
John to Jamie

MY FAVOURITE BOOK

Spring is always a good time for renewal. Here we are, starting a new season, with the days getting longer and brighter. I've been thinking about a book I need to reread, to renew my acquaintance with it.

The first exercise I ever devised for a writing workshop began with the question, 'What's your favourite book?' The exercise remains absolutely fundamental to my workshops because I believe we need to read better if we are to write better. Often I'm asked what my favourite book might be and I usually reply, F. Scott Fitzgerald's *The Great Gatsby*. It is a wonderful book but it's an answer given for convenience. People generally nod and understand whereas if I said my real favourite....

Now I have to name it. For a reason, it's been forced on me by a piece of news. You might have seen that, 40 years on, a shortlist of six novels has been published for the 'lost' Booker Prize of 1970. There was a mix-up at the time which meant that several months worth of novels published that year were not even considered for the Booker. The chosen shortlist is a fine one: it includes Muriel Spark and Nina Bawden, and JG Farrell's brilliant *Troubles*. It also includes my favourite book: *The Vivisector* by Patrick White.

People tend to ask, who? I'm used to that response, even though Patrick White won the Nobel Prize for Literature in 1973. He was an Australian novelist and playwright, isolated geographically from the rest of the world, but isolated temperamentally, too. He never sought fame. When he was offered it in the form of the Nobel Prize, he asked his friend, the painter Sydney Nolan, to collect it for him. And now the world seems to have shunned Patrick White as he once shunned the world. But we really should not. His novels are magnificent.

The prickliness of his own character comes through in his novels. All Patrick White's characters are outsiders; they are outside society but inside life. He himself was uneasy as a social being. A gay man in a macho society, he had no affection for much of the life he observed around him. His characters become heroic simply by surviving, they have a life force that is the essence of humanity.

The books are now often described as unfashionable, perhaps because the characters have no small talk. They talk, and small statements take on immense significance. Individual words have an enormous emotional charge. This gives each book a monumental, epic scale; they are big books, books of over-reaching ambition, but he despised life when it was lived meanly or pettily.

This made him an uncompromising character, and an uncompromising writer who made no concessions to popular taste. He championed the human instinct to survive against all the odds, while seeking and celebrating a majesty in that instinct. Sometimes the instinct showed itself as a single-minded obsession, sometimes as artistic imagination. Perhaps the character who embodies this most is Hurtle Duffield, whose life story forms *The Vivisector*.

Hurtle rises above his human weaknesses through his own creativity. He is a painter (partly modelled on Sydney Nolan) and he expresses his feelings for the world through his paintings. There are extraordinary descriptions of those paintings, of the Australian landscape and of a gallery of strange, flawed characters. It's a big book in every sense but when I first read it I couldn't stop reading it, so powerful was its imaginative grip. I'll be reading it again this summer.

I think it's important to read. It's the best advice I can give any writer: to read as widely as possible. As part of that reading we should all read 'big' books occasionally, not just the easy-reads.

Is there a big book that you've always meant to read? Perhaps one that you've resisted reading? Make a resolution to read that book. Persevere. Then write a review of it.

Jamie to John

WHY FICTION?

This reminds me of a conversation we had last autumn on our annual trip to Andalucia for the Dark Angels advanced course. 'Why should I read fiction?' asked one of the students. It seemed like a good question, and a reminder for me that not everyone has the passion for stories that you and I share with our fellow Dark Angels tutor, Stuart Delves.

People read for many reasons. It may be to learn or to become better informed, it may simply be for entertainment, and it doesn't have to involve fiction. Even if people do read novels, it may not be for any reason other than to be caught up in a good yarn.

Nevertheless, the question invited us to reflect on the fact that there are deeper reasons for reading fiction; and since it was seriously put it deserved a serious answer. I seem to remember that you and I hit our stride quickly. Because it helps you to see the world around you in a new light, we replied; because it reveals universal truths; because it highlights moral dilemmas; because it reflects what it means to be human; because it stretches your heart and mind; because it challenges your view of things; because it helps you develop and grow; and so on.

But what have such reflections got to do with business writing? After all, isn't that about facts and the hard realities of commercial or organisational life? Well, yes. But to whom do those facts and hard realities apply? People. People whose lives, wherever they are, at home or at work, involve searching for universal truths, facing moral dilemmas, reflecting on what it means to be human, developing and growing, and so on. I rest my case…

Just the other day I was asked a different question, yet one which goes hand-in-hand with the first: 'How do I become a better writer? Would reading help? And if so, what? Newspapers, novels…?'

My reply, of course, echoed your thoughts closely. Yes, I said, and yes again. Reading does help; in fact it's probably the best way there is to become a better writer. Reading something that seems to be well written — journalism, fiction, non-fiction, the genre really doesn't matter — is surely an invitation to anyone with the least curiosity to investigate how it's done. Syntax, vocabulary, rhythm, texture, colour, energy — all can be learnt from what we read, and the more we read the sooner we start breathing it in.

But most importantly of all, reading — for either the story or the style — teaches us that the best writers, in any field whatsoever, are those that are deeply preoccupied with being human. For them, making the connection is everything. And why would we not want to do that in our working lives? Writing better can help us.

94 THINGS TO DO

Pick a day and read the main leader in one of the broadsheet newspapers and one of the tabloids (ideally if they're on the same topic) and compare them. Think about how they were crafted. What are the writers doing to make their points? What can you learn from them? Which newspaper do you think is more effective?

Week 15
John to Jamie

STORY TIME

You ended with newspaper stories. We're used to the word in that context. But it's become a little fashionable to use the word 'storytelling' in business. The truth is, it can mean any number of things. I discovered this, slightly uncomfortably, a couple of years ago when John Mitchinson (a former client at Waterstone's and now co-founder of QI) invited me to speak at a storytelling conference he had helped organise at Cumberland Lodge.

I found myself one of three speakers in the late afternoon session. The first speaker talked about the uses of storytelling in education, particularly with children who experience learning difficulties because of family backgrounds, unfamiliarity with English, and so on. The second speaker talked about the therapeutic uses of storytelling in social work, particularly with patients experiencing deep grief. It was emotional stuff.

Then it was my turn to talk about storytelling in business. Or, as it could easily be seen by that audience, how to make money by deceiving people. Anyway, I soldiered on. In a business context, what stories do best is explain what a particular company or brand is about — what drives it, what motivates its people. Businesses try to do that with mission statements and brand definitions, but it is stories that make the connections with people's emotions. I told tales of Guinness, Nike and Starbucks, but no one attacked me. They're brands with good stories, with strong narrative themes — for Guinness it's 'Reflects your inner strength'; Nike 'Just do it'; Starbucks 'Rewarding everyday moments'. The stories they tell everyday — in advertising, promotions, point of sale — reflect those themes.

The truth is, it did make sense to put those different kinds of storytelling together in one session. As human beings perhaps one of the most fundamental things that unites us is a love of storytelling. It's more universal than, say, liking the music of

Michael Jackson, or enjoying an ice cream on a sunny beach, or feeling involved in the drama of a football match.

Storytelling is particularly important for businesses because the individual work we do is a story. It's what gives each of us an identity. When we go off to work each day we are creating a new narrative. There might be similarities in the story from one day to another — you might always catch the 7.21 a.m. train from Pangbourne to Paddington. But the story will always be different because different people, actions and thoughts change the daily story.

But good businesses tell good stories. And they encourage their people to create good stories with an enlightened attitude. This means allowing people to use their initiative and encouraging their creativity rather than tying everyone down to the equivalent of a call centre script. Jeff Bezos, founder of Amazon, expressed it like this: 'Your brand is what people say about you when you're not in the room'. You have to recognise that as a business you can't control every element of every story. So learn to enjoy them instead.

93 THINGS TO DO

Think of a brand that you often buy. Why do you choose it? If the price of another similar product were much cheaper would you still choose your favoured brand? How would you write that brand's story? Write about your relationship with that brand, using details from your own life. What do you think is the essence of that brand? See if you can use that definition to shape the way you write the story.

Jamie to John

VALUE ADDED

You mentioned Nike and their message, 'Just do it'. The story goes that the founder, Bill Bowerman, experimented with his wife's waffle iron when he first had the idea for a revolutionary running shoe with an indented sole. For everyone but his wife it was a triumph, a masterpiece of improvisation. The iron was there to hand when he needed it. He just did it — and ruined the iron in the process.

Founding stories are often very revealing about businesses. Invariably they're human stories (because that's the only kind there is), and invariably they involve some kind of struggle or tale of obstacles overcome (because business success is never won easily). So, directly or indirectly they end up telling us a lot about what the founders believed in and stood for.

I've always loved the Innocent drinks brand founding story, which you tell in your book in the *Great Brand Stories* series, John. The three founders tested their prototype smoothies at a music festival. Above their stall was a banner asking: 'Should we give up our day jobs?' In front of it were two big black bins for empty bottles. One had written on it 'Yes', the other 'No'. At the end of the weekend, the Yes bin was full — so they went to their jobs next day and resigned. The story speaks of a certain innocent belief in the quality of the product, which still permeates the brand today.

These stories work because they speak about brands or businesses in non-business terms. A friend of mine is an inspirational figure called Jim Adamson who founded a Scottish video production and events management company. He's inspiring for many reasons, but mainly because he's a paraplegic who lost the use of his legs under extraordinary circumstances. I thought his personal story spoke volumes about his company's values and I persuaded him to let me tell it. This is how it began:

Against the odds

Every business has a founding story. Ours may not be quite what you expected.

Jim Adamson was an ordinary apprentice in the Scottish Highlands. Then in 1966, he had a life-changing experience. He was accidentally shot in the throat and paralysed.

For most people it would have been the end. For Jim, it was just the beginning. He went to university, got several degrees and discovered a new talent. He was exceptionally good at making television programmes...

Jim doesn't want anyone's sympathy and Speakeasy, his business, certainly doesn't need it; it does very well. But my contention was that people's connection with the company would be strengthened and deepened by knowing something of its founder's personal struggle to overcome his physical limitations, the self-belief he needed to build a successful business. It made it a more interesting place. You could say it gave it personality.

92 THINGS TO DO

Ask a few colleagues or friends to tell you stories of their personal triumphs or disasters at work. What do those stories reveal of the tellers' personal values? Try retelling one of them in such a way that it also says something about the values of the organisation in question.

Week 16
John to Jamie

IT'S A MYTH

It's certainly a myth that only 'serious' writing, using lots of abstract nouns and dry objectivity, gives you authority. In fact, the opposite is true because such writing leads to pomposity on your part and incomprehension on your reader's part — and those effects undermine any authority you might have been striving for.

Perhaps the opposite style to this kind of business-speak is mythology itself, and you mention our shared interest. I've always loved the Greek and Roman myths in particular. This week I've been researching the myths of Apollo for a book of stories I'm writing. I came across the story of Apollo using a white crow — in those days all crows were white — to keep watch on his lover Coronis. The crow observed Coronis' infidelity but did nothing to stop it and nothing to revenge it. Enraged, Apollo turned the crow, and all crows, forever black.

What's the relevance of that to business writing? Well, I guarantee that you will now remember the story the next time you see a crow. And that's a powerful effect to achieve with a piece of writing. When was the last time you read a paragraph of business writing that had the same impact?

But what I really love about mythology is that those stories were invented to explain the workings of a complex, often baffling world. They deal in fundamental emotions and ideas, personified in the characters of gods and people. They give us insights into universal human hopes, fears and motivations. They are very clear about purpose and theme. All these qualities are essential — but too often missing — in business communication.

We agree about the power of stories, recognizing that the narrative structures of myths tell us much about how writing works. And in workshops we use those structures to give clarity and direction to writing.

Without being slavish to such structural descriptions they can help set a useful framework for writing. I've recently suggested three-part storytelling forms to a big accountancy firm and a supermarket retailer. In simple terms it's Challenge–Exploration – Resolution. This works on the level of the individual paragraph and a longer piece. Here's the founding story of the RSA 'translated' into that same narrative form by me recently.

Enlightenment

It was a time of exciting ideas. There was an excitement about ideas that could make life better, an intellectual buzz across Europe and the world.

In a coffee house in London William Shipley discussed with like-minded individuals how to change society for the public good. He founded the RSA in that coffee house in 1754. The RSA's grown and developed since then, throwing up a stream of pioneering ideas about education, the environment, business, the arts — bringing about constructive change.

The RSA's belief in the power of many minds is stronger today than ever. It's turning imaginative thinking into practical action: 21st century Enlightenment.

I'm sure these storytelling structures come from the natural rhythms of life. The seasons. Dawn and dusk, day and night. For example, if we were to describe the narrative structure of *Room 121* in terms of the seasonal cycle we might put it like this:

1. Winter — Laying in stores
2. Spring — Sowing seeds
3. Summer — Nurturing growth
4. Autumn — Reaping the harvest

91 THINGS TO DO

Think of a story or myth that you know well. Retell that story in four different ways, changing details to fit the changing moods of the seasons. Start each retelling in a different season, and end it in another season, changing your story to reflect this difference. What happens if you end it in, say, spring rather than winter? Does the tragic turn into something more hopeful and romantic?

Jamie to John

THE CHILD WITHIN

The Bible contains what is probably the most famous story ever told, at least in the Judaeo-Christian world. One of the authors I will be interviewing later on in the summer, at the Edinburgh

International Book Festival, is the world-famous linguistics professor, David Crystal. His new book is the wonderfully titled *Begat*, about the influence of the King James Bible on the English language.

The book features the 257 Biblical expressions (fewer than he expected when he began his research, he admits) that in one form or another have found their way into the common parlance: expressions such as 'fly in the ointment', 'my brother's keeper', 'east of Eden' and so on.

Along with *Begat*, his publishers also sent me another new book of his, *A Little Book of Language*. It describes our relationship with language from our very first infant cry to the way we develop our own distinctive 'voice' as adults. It's simply and charmingly written, illustrated with pleasing woodcuts, full of fascinating information ('salary' and 'sausage' have the same etymological root, for example) and peppered with did-you-know pages featuring talking parrots, rhyming slang, foreign language texting and the like.

But it left me with a question: who was it written for? There was nothing on the jacket to say it was for foreigners or children, but there was something in the voice that nagged at me. I did a little digging and discovered that he had actually written it for 12 year olds. Yet this was a book that would entertain and inform any adult reader. In fact, my bet is that one would learn much more about language from this little volume than from any weighty textbook.

As it happens, an exercise I often set people in workshops is to describe what they do as if writing to a 12-year-old. It gets them away from all the default words and phrases which, I often joke, live and breed in the air conditioning of most big organisations. In doing so, it forces them to think about what those clichés really mean and then find simpler ways to explain them.

But the really interesting thing about the results is that far from sounding dumbed-down or childish, they usually sound clear and simple and almost always more meaningful. I once heard the former Children's Laureate, Michael Morpurgo, say that the adults he found most interesting were the ones who know that the child inside them is their soul. One of the things that children crave, in this world of ever-increasing complexity, is simplicity. And that child is in all of us. We should remember it when we write at work.

90 THINGS TO DO

Can you describe what you do as if writing for a 12-year-old? If you've got one of your own, try it out on them. If not, borrow someone else's. Encourage them to ask questions. Make sure they really understand. Then write down your description. Would it work for adults? What does it tell you?

Week 17
John to Jamie

IN DREAMS

It's one of the great joys we've both experienced recently — a first grandchild, and at an age when we're still young enough to enjoy the experience. Seeing Aimee learn to communicate is wonderful, and certainly helps to connect with 'the child inside'. Another way we do this is through dreams.

Every dream is a new story, created in an individual mind. The other week Harry Pearce, partner at Pentagram and one of my most regular collaborators, told me about the way he records his dreams. It began with an interest in Jung more than 20 years ago and now he keeps a dream journal, writing down (in the middle of the night) the dream he has just had. In the daytime he will expand the story from memory and, when it seems right, illustrate it, too.

All this is top of my mind because I'm writing these words as I fly home from Istanbul. I'm sitting in a cramped aircraft seat, remembering in an almost dreamlike way, some of the places in Turkey I've seen in the last week. Almost mythical places, like Troy and Ephesus.

I remember we'd had cups of coffee in the Grand Bazaar the day before. The Illy cups had the word 'dream' written on them in several different languages. It occurred to me that dreaming is the most universal of all human activities — it is perhaps what makes us human. And I remember a Milan Kundera quotation: 'Our dreams prove that to imagine — to dream about things that have not happened — is among mankind's deepest needs.'

Earlier in the week we'd visited the ancient site at Pergamon in western Turkey. Here, they had once housed one of the ancient world's largest collections of writings. Pergamon gives us the word 'parchment', the form of paper on which they wrote. The fortress, palace and library were sited on the acropolis but down below was the Asklepion, the ancient medical centre, with its snake symbol. 'Identity' is not a modern business invention.

In the third century BC, people came here to be treated in ways that now seem very new age. Therapies of various kinds helped healing, using herbs, aromas and theatrical performance. You can stand in the domed building and see the evidence of the dream chambers. Recognizing the recuperative power of sleep and dreams, doctors would speak quietly through cavities in the walls, aiming to influence the dreams of sleepers with positive thoughts.

Now, as I write, the plane is over the English Channel and I'm nearly home. I think of a story that John Sorrell told me just before my holiday. He'd visited the painter Terry Frost in Cornwall towards the end of the artist's life. John had asked him about the new painting positioned above the TV. Terry Frost explained that this was where he placed his current work. He liked to doze in front of the TV. When he woke up the painting would be the first thing he saw and sometimes the painting would catch him 'unawares'. In doing so, it would look right or not, finished or still a work in the process of creation. He found this the best test.

I loved that idea, the thought of waking from a dream and immediately making a decision. Deciding when a piece of writing is complete is always a hard call to make. Right — or not? Genuine or fake? We can all dream.

At the end of the conversation with Harry Pearce we decided on the approach for the new identity for International PEN. Sometimes, you just have to relax and let the idea emerge in its own way, like a dream. It's all about 'processing information'. Sleep on it. You'll see it with fresh eyes in the morning light.

89 THINGS TO DO

For the next few days make a conscious effort to remember your dreams. Write them down and see what new writing and ideas emerge. Perhaps you'll find a use for a word, a phrase or a story to feed into your writing at work.

Jamie to John

FREEWHEELING

For me it's while having a morning shower that I make those intuitive leaps and connections. There's something about standing there, still half asleep, with the hot water pounding the back of my neck that puts me into the zone. An 'alpha brainwave state' is the technical term, I think — a kind of waking dreaming, as you say.

Other people find that place driving or walking or listening to music or working with their hands. It's whatever puts your mind into neutral, allows it to freewheel, so that there's room for those ideas to surface freely from the subconscious where they've been secretly turning over. For me it's often the moment when the 'hook' for something I have to write emerges from the welter of information I've collected at the research stage.

A year or so ago I was asked to write a student recruitment ad for my alma mater, Aberdeen University. I've done a lot of writing for the university over the years, mainly on the fund-raising and development side, so my mental database is stuffed with information about the place. But at the time it just seemed like a mess of porridge that wouldn't yield anything of interest.

Then, standing in the shower, I got it. I would tell the story of the bishop who founded the university in 1495, whose vision and perseverance paid off and is echoed today, more than 500 years later, by the current leaders who have international ambitions for their university, and the students who come to Aberdeen to work hard and get good degrees. It began like this:

Of grit and granite

A 15th century bishop had a dream. If his northerly, granite-built town could educate its own professionals, its prosperity would surely grow. But he needed money and royal consent.

So he talked to the king and his nobles, his friends in the church, the city fathers and merchants. His determination was unquenchable.

And here we are, back with dreams and stories again! Once you've experienced their power, it's surprisingly difficult to stay away from them. They work, as we've both already said more than once, because they're human and therefore charged with emotion, and you can't tell them in business speak. But there's something else that's crucial for me in all storytelling. I learnt it first through writing my novels and now I'm always conscious of it, whatever I write.

It's what you might call the 'significant detail', the little gem of information, sometimes almost inconsequential-seeming, that brings the writing to life and makes its subject real. I once interviewed an old fiddle-maker who showed me a caliper he'd made from the metal heel of his boot, a piece of an old steel ruler, a welding rod and the top of a tube of eye ointment. Writers dream of that kind of information because it's impossible to make up.

In your description of Pergamon the significant detail is the symbol of the snake on the Asklepion. It leaves a picture in my mind. In my bishop's tale, it's the image of him going to talk to the city fathers and merchants. I can see prosperous, bearded men in furs holding solemn conversations in their cold granite city. These images carry feelings with them. They lodge much more deeply than plain facts and I reach for them every time I pick up my pencil.

88 THINGS TO DO

What puts you into the zone? Once you're aware of it you can make use of it, get to know it and trust that it will deliver for you. Try and visit it as regularly as you can. And let it help you mine your research for the little gleaming nugget, the significant detail, that will bring what you write alive.

Week 18
John to Jamie

MEMORY GOING FORWARD

It's an interesting question: where does inspiration come from? How do we get the stimulus to write something that really connects to the imaginations of others? What is imagination?

I increasingly think of imagination as a muscle. We need to exercise it to keep it alive. I'm sure neither of us believes that ideas drop out of a clear blue sky to refresh a blessed few. The harder you work your imagination, the stronger it becomes.

It's why we run our workshops and why they succeed. I'm thinking about exercises we do in Spain, for example, involving storytelling from the Spanish language. It sounds impossible but people rise to the challenge. How? At its best it's a matter of looking outwards, drawing on things unfamiliar, this foreign language, this alien landscape. And at the same time looking inwards to your own memories, your own personality.

I think particularly of the stories I wrote to reflect the Guinness brand and its essence of 'inner strength'. I stumbled upon an exhibition in Trinity College, Dublin, about manuscripts illuminated by medieval monks, and it unlocked everything for me.

Recently I ran a series of business writing workshops for Orange. I asked the poet Maura Dooley along to read her work and talk to the assembled group of marketing and communications people. She inspired them to think differently about their writing, and her reading sent me back to her poems. So I read one of her poems called 'Future Memory'. The title appealed. It included this quotation from Lewis Carroll's *Alice Through the Looking Glass:* 'It's a poor sort of memory that only works backwards', the Queen remarked.

This related to one of my beliefs. People often say apprehensively before a workshop: 'I'm not creative. I've not got much imagination.' I always insist: 'Oh yes you have.' So I do a particular exercise that is about memory — no one can disagree that we all have a memory. It then becomes clear that memory and imagination are siblings; they share origins and perhaps they often come together in dreams. Do we really remember all the details of something that has happened? Are we really imagining what we remember, or are we remembering what we have in fact imagined?

This also reminded me that a client at the National Australia Bank had sent me an article just before the workshop. It was by the Financial Times' Lucy Kellaway, scourge of bad writing in business. The phrase 'going forward' was the target of her scorn, and I agree that it can be irritatingly meaningless as a substitute for, or addition to, positive noises about the future.

But let's not chuck out 'going forward' altogether. I prefer to go forward than to go backward: you're less likely to fall over. I also like the idea of having a memory that goes forward as well as backward. I guess that *memory going forward* could be called *imagination*.

Think back to last Sunday morning. What were you doing? How did you feel when you woke up? What was the weather like? Now think back to your first day at school. What can you remember? Who was with you? What were you wearing? Write down as much as you can remember, even if the memories are vague. Then think: have you been using your memory or your imagination?

Jamie to John

A FEW KIND WORDS

Here's a memory of a moment that has given me impetus, that's got me going forward you might say, for several years now. In fact, looking back on it, I realise that it was one of the most important moments of my recent career.

We were at Moniack Mhor, the writer's centre in Inverness-shire, running a Dark Angels course. It was breakfast time on the last day and that evening everyone, including you and me, were going to read out a piece they had written. The only problem was that so far we, the tutors, had not had time to write anything. That was coming in the afternoon.

As I was standing by the toaster, cup of tea in hand, wondering sleepily what I might write about, something surfaced that had first struck me the previous summer. I'd heard Adam Philips, the writer and psychiatrist, being interviewed at the Edinburgh International Book Festival. He was talking about modern malaises of the spirit, and arguing that we need to be kinder to one another.

The word 'kind', as we use it today to mean sympathetic or compassionate, he pointed out, is derived from the word 'kind' meaning of the same kind, or kin, as in 'mankind'. So when, in bygone times, we met someone from our own village or clan or tribe, we were predisposed to be 'kind' to one another in the sense that we were related and therefore understood one another. We had the same reference points and could communicate easily. We had no reason to be suspicious of one another and every reason to help one another out.

The kitchen radio was on as I stood waiting for my toast to pop. It was Friday morning and presenter Sue Lawley was quizzing a gravel-voiced American soprano, Renée Fleming, on Desert Island Discs. The diva was talking about travelling and working around the world. The idea of kindness was turning in my mind and I wasn't really listening, but suddenly I heard words that leapt out at me: 'The kindness of strangers'.

And there, in one of those serendipitous moments that bring meaning and delight to the apparent chaos of our world, I had a title for my piece and a theme to follow. It turned into a poem about the common humanity we had shared on the course. But it didn't stop there, because the more I thought about it the more I realised that we should all be aware of that 'kindness' whenever we communicate, that it's how we make the best connections.

Today it's my mantra, and even the title of my blog: 'A few kind words'. I talk constantly about how we must remember when we write that we are all humankind, that whoever reads our words will be someone probably very like us, so we need to be 'kinder' to one another. The alternative, a speciality of the business word, is to be 'unkind' — and that doesn't make for good communication.

86 THINGS TO DO

When you next have to write something, picture the person you're writing to if you can. Imagine them reading what you're writing. If you don't personally know your reader or readers, imagine a typical one, give them a name and picture them somewhere, their home or place of work. Are they engaged by what you're saying?

ON AN INNOCENT THEME

I went off to judge the D&AD 'Writing for design' awards last week. I was foreman of the jury and we'd voted secretly on what work — if any — deserved the top award, a Yellow Pencil. A Yellow Pencil is the Oscar of the creative business world. We awarded it to Innocent Drinks for the words and design on their 1-litre smoothie packs.

During the judging day I was impressed by my fellow jurors' analysis of Innocent's contribution to our world of communication and writing. As foreman, I'd tried to stand back a little from the debate — after all, I've written the book on Innocent — but listened as others gave Innocent their due. This means that I can now say that the award was richly deserved. Innocent have changed the landscape for all of us who are writers for design, writers for business.

This morning I popped into Sainsbury's and bought a 1-litre Innocent smoothie. It was lemon, honey and ginger, not one of those submitted to the awards (it's a new flavour). It seems to me to express so much of what makes Innocent successful. It needs a long essay but I'm not going to write it here, so let's just take one line, in yellow type on a black silhouette of a bee hive: 'Buy one get one bee'. The line made me smile, as Innocent often do, but behind every smile there is always the single-minded purpose that I'd express as: 'This is about giving you a fruit drink that's as natural as we can make it.'

It's a worthy message but delivered in a completely disarming way. They acknowledge their place in the commercial world by subverting the wording of the 'buy one get one free' message you see on every high street. But what really matters is that it's not done for the sake of the joke but to focus our attention harder than ever on the cause. Bees are disappearing. If they do, it will be a natural catastrophe. So let's do something about it. It's this ability to concentrate on their own narrative theme, never deviating, that drives all of Innocent's language and storytelling. That is increasingly hard to do, and even harder to sustain, and Innocent have been doing it now for a dozen years.

We can learn a lesson from that, but let's learn the right lesson. There have been too many briefs coming from the driest and most corporate of quarters, saying 'Write it like Innocent'. By that they mean, 'Make us sound like human beings'. But the fact is, you should sound like Innocent only if you are Innocent. Their success is down to their single-minded adhesion to their narrative theme. It starts and continues with the name itself, but you see it in everything they do. It's fruit and nothing but fruit: do only natural things.

If you're an accountancy firm, for example, I really don't think that's your theme, so you wouldn't want an Innocent tone. The lesson to learn is that you should define your company's distinctive purpose, express it as your brand's story and tell it with words that fit the theme.

85 THINGS TO DO

Go to the websites of three well-known brands. Read their home pages and some of their descriptions of themselves. Ask yourself: is there a clear, consistent theme? How do they express it? How would you express it?

Jamie to John

THIS IS BAD ENOUGH

'Make us sound like human beings.' It's a sentiment echoed almost exactly by my friend Elspeth Murray in her fine poem *This Is Bad Enough* (see p.83).

Elspeth is a live wire with language, a poet who worked for a long time in the health service as a project manager. We came together a few years ago to run workshops with groups of doctors, healthcare workers and former cancer patients. The object was to consider how to improve the information that people receive at different stages along the cancer 'journey'.

We looked at examples which ranged from the friendly and informative to the virtually unintelligible, the simple to the terrifying. The one thing that many of them had in common was a tendency to speak in the clinical, rather peremptory, often condescending and largely masculine language of the consultant physician. What an equally large number lacked was any kind of empathy. And this, remember, in leaflets some of which were destined for readers who had just heard the worst news of their lives.

After a while Elspeth moved on to write more poetry and help her husband with his hugely successful puppet show, 'The Man Who Planted Trees'. I carried on with the workshops and a few months ago I received an e-mail from one of the participants, an oncologist, enclosing a copy of a leaflet that she and her team had subsequently written 'in a very different style from the one it would have been without your input'.

It was clear, direct, warm, empathetic, authoritative, helpful and respectful. It treated the readers as human beings, it subtly acknowledged their predicament and it spoke to them as equals. I could scarcely fault it and I don't mind admitting that it made me feel immensely proud. Here's a short excerpt:

> *There are a lot of different drugs that can be used to control nausea or vomiting. Sometimes it can be difficult to swallow these if you are feeling full up. Do let your specialist know if you are struggling or if you cannot manage your tablets. Even something as simple as changing to liquids instead of tablets can help but there are also drugs that dissolve in your mouth that may help.*

When you read this, it doesn't conjure images of white coats or stethoscopes. Which is not, alas, generally true of the NHS. It has mountainous lessons to learn about language, as anyone will know who has ever been summoned in writing to a hospital appointment ('you are required to attend …'), let alone been handed a 'patient information' leaflet on any subject.

The lessons can be learnt, of course, but the starting point, the absolute foundation of any learning when it comes to writing about health, is that language must be part of the healing process. As my oncologist friend demonstrated so well, it just takes a little imagination, a bit of graft, and the will to connect. The opposite doesn't really bear thinking about.

84 THINGS TO DO

We all sometimes come across official language that seems particularly insensitive to the reader's feelings. Next time you see something like this, try rewriting it as one human being to another, as if you really wanted to help the reader and make them feel better.

This Is Bad Enough
By Elspeth Murray

This is bad enough
So please …

Don't give me
gobbledegook.

Don't give me
pages and dense pages
and
'this leaflet aims to explain…'

Don't give me
really dodgy photocopying
and
'DO NOT REMOVE
FOR REFERENCE ONLY.'

Don't give me
'drafted in collaboration with
a multidisciplinary stakeholder
partnership consultation
short-life project working group.'
I mean is this about
you guys
or me?

This is hard enough
So please:

Don't leave me
oddly none the wiser or
listening till my eyes are
glazing over.

Don't leave me
wondering what on earth that was about,
feeling like it's rude to ask
or consenting to goodness knows what.

Don't leave me
lost in another language
adrift in bad translation.

Don't leave me
chucking it in the bin
Don't leave me
leaving in the state I'm in.

Don't leave me
feeling even more clueless
than I did before any of this
happened.

This is tough enough
So please:

Make it relevant,
understandable —

or reasonably
readable
at least.

Why not put in
pictures
or sketches,
or something to
guide me through?

I mean how hard can it be
for the people
who are steeped in this stuff
to keep it up-to-date?

And you know what I'd appreciate?
A little time to take it in
a little time to show them at home
a little time to ask 'What's that?'
a little time to talk on the phone.

So give us
the clarity, right from the start
the contacts, there at the end.

Give us the info
you know we need to know.
Show us the facts,
some figures
And don't forget our feelings.

Because this is bad
and hard

and tough enough
so please speak
like a human
Make it better
not worse.

From John to Jamie

TO WRITE IS HUMAN

Elspeth's poem is magnificent in its humanity. Alongside this, I think of another aspect of humanity — Wendi Aarons' explosion of rage at Proctor & Gamble's condescending language in the packaging of 'feminine products'. This is part of the letter she sent to P&G's (male) brand manager for that category.

> *Last month, while in the throes of cramping so painful I wanted to reach inside my body and yank out my uterus, I opened an Always maxi-pad, and there, printed on the adhesive backing, were these words: 'Have a Happy Period.'*
>
> *Are you f— kidding me? What I mean is, does any part of your tiny middle-manager brain really think happiness — actual smiling, laughing happiness, is possible during a menstrual period?*

You have to use your own skills of human empathy to judge the effect of your own writing. When you let it go its own way into the world you can be fairly certain that your words will be read by another human being. It's why we've called this book *Room 121* — it's about writing as a human being to a human being.

There are some people who wish this wasn't so. The story on Channel 4 News last week was presented as a bit of fun but actually it's worrying that computer programs are now used to mark some English exams. The Chartered Institute of Educational Assessors tried out one of these programs, developed in the US, and tested some famous writers with it.

A passage of Hemingway failed the computer test for its 'lack of care in style of writing'. They then tried Golding's *Lord of the Flies*, much read in schools, represented by this line:

> *You could see a knee disturb the mould. Now the other. Two hands. A Spear. A Face.*

The computer judged this as having 'inaccurate and erratic sentence structure'. While Winston Churchill was sent to the back of the class for promising to 'fight on the beaches' then going on to 'fight on the landing grounds, we shall fight in the fields and in the streets'. This, of course, was dismissed as 'too repetitive'.

If we fight against judgement by computer — in the offices, in the classrooms, in the streets — what are the means we should use to judge ourselves? Of course, there's no easy answer. But perhaps one test that separates us from computers (at least for now) and makes us human, is our ability to listen to the sound of our words and follow our emotions as a result. We always use that test in our workshops. I like to think that the P&G brand manager, listening to 'Have a Happy Period', would have squirmed uncomfortably as he said it and disposed of it in a suitable waste bag.

83 THINGS TO DO

Try running some of your words through a computer-based program like the Microsoft Readability Index. See what score your words get. You might not want to take the score too seriously because this will be judging your writing on limited criteria. But it will also tell you what the criteria are. Judge for yourself which of the criteria are important to your writing.

Jamie to John

MURDER BY PROCESS

Viola Tors wanted more community involvement, public hearings, more transparency, a poll, an environmental impact study … She was a killer of wonderful ideas and like so many murderers, she used procedure as a weapon.

Viola Tors features in the novel *Liberty*, a recent tale from Lake Wobegon by that wise observer of human foibles, Garrison Keillor.

A member of her local Fourth of July committee, Viola hails from small-town Minnesota. But one suspects she would be quite at home in the offices of any one of those big organisations where, on any given day, following detailed consultation with partners and stakeholders, major strategies are being identified, designed and implemented in order to initiate short-life project working groups tasked with significant action plans.

There are two problems here. One is that these processes may be necessary, they may even be essential, but that doesn't mean they make for exciting reading. Expecting people outside your organisation to be interested in its procedures is like asking a perfect stranger to take an interest in the workings of your large intestine. Yet forests are felled, web pages without number are written, in order that these rumblings of the corporate gut can be broadcast to the world at large.

Why? Who honestly cares? What most of us want to know about organisations we don't belong to (even those we do belong to) is: what do they do in the real world? What benefits do they bring to society, if they're in the public sector? What benefits do their goods or services bring to me, if they're in business? The processes that allow them to function are nothing more than the *sine qua non* of working life. And to make a virtue of them leaves us wondering: do these organisations maybe have nothing else to offer?

(In the commercial world, product features often become a kind of analogy for processes. Technology businesses in particular bombard customers with information about the clever stuff their gadgets can do, when what most people want to know is how the gadgets can improve their lives. When I was helping to run a series of workshops for BT, one of the points we made was that people would generally rather know the new phone means they don't have to remember their mum's number, rather than that it comes with a 250-address pre-storable digital contacts book.)

But back to processes … the other, bigger problem is that behind them there are always real people, more often than not with real conviction, doing real things. But because the language of procedure is so abstract, you would never know it. Indeed, it's sometimes quite hard to figure out what the organisation in question actually does. And wherever the language of process is allowed to stifle the language of purpose, you can be fairly sure that somewhere not far off there's the dismal sound of creativity being strangled — and Viola Tors sharpening her pencil.

82 THINGS TO DO

Next time you have to write about what your organisation does, think hard about who is going to read it. Do they really need to know about how you do what you do? And if they do, can you describe it in a real rather than an abstract way? Rather than telling us how 'the strategy will be identified, developed and implemented', tell us what you're actually planning to do: for example, planting tulips on the roundabouts.

Week 21

John to Jamie

FINDING THE IDEA

I suspect Viola Tors is now feeling puzzled, Jamie. She finds comfort in her process, just as the technology geek is comforted by product features. They're comforted by the thought that only they, and a few like-minded others, can understand those things. Actually, the process and the procedures don't matter nearly as much as the purpose and the benefit. But purpose and benefits need clarity.

Some people use procedure as a way of ordering the world but avoiding the clarity of an idea. But how do you find that idea? Surely there must be a process? Research is central to the process but by research I don't mean focus groups or number-crunching analysis. I just mean finding out more about a subject: reading, talking, observing, immersing yourself to find things that are new to you. If you're delighted by the discovery, the chances are your readers will be, too.

The current '26 Treasures' project at the V&A is a good example. We have a good idea. The development of the idea is a convoluted tale of a couple of writers (one of them me) reading, making a connection, sharing with someone to make a further connection, doing a little research, including a visit to the V&A, then finally beginning to write. We then put the idea to the V&A: they grasped it immediately, and here we are — 26 writers — working with one of the world's great galleries. Our aim is to engage visitors with objects in the gallery through our words.

The curator of the British Galleries at the V&A has chosen 26 different objects that were designed and made between the years 1500 and 1760. We then randomly paired those objects with 26 writers — drawing names written on paper from a plastic cup. So all of a sudden you find you have a new interest in, say, 18th century Rococo candle stands. Just as a new client might contact you about a business you've never had any contact with, to write about a new product you know nothing about. You have to find out, and the search is part of the excitement of writing because it involves thinking. And from the apparent complexity you find a simpler idea that means something personal to you.

From a collection of millions of objects we are focusing on just 26. Yet, in a strange way, that element of randomness (why those 26 treasures with those 26 writers?) is a true reflection of life. The internet now puts so much information at our disposal yet how little of it do we actually access? It's a task beyond the human brain to reach every crevice of the internet, or every nook and cranny of the V&A.

So '26 Treasures' is a random snapshot, but I think it's all the more realistic for being so. What this randomness shows is that we can all be inspired to write by an object, any object. It's not the 26 treasures that are universal, it's the nature of inspiration. The project is an exploration of inspiration, demonstrating that there is always an element of randomness — serendipity, if you like — in every act of creation. Or perhaps that's what we really mean by individuality? All individuals react in their own ways to the random acts that make life. Those reactions create stories.

The V&A project makes clear that there is a process after all. But it's a process that needs quick thinking in response to apparent randomness.

81 THINGS TO DO

Set aside 30 minutes. Open a dictionary at random and read the definition of the word you're looking at. Find out as much as you can about that word in the first 20 minutes, using other books and the Internet. In the last 10 minutes of your time, use automatic writing to record your response to your discoveries.

Jamie to John

SIMPLICITY RULES, OK?

Sceptical observers would say that the world of high finance is a pretty random one, as close to science as a spin at the roulette table, and that financiers apply processes to it *post facto* in order to make it look as if they exercise some control, whereas in fact they mostly have none.

It certainly suits them to present their world as a complex one. Having written over the years for many banks, investment managers and insurance companies, I've often been left wondering whether they really want to have their business simplified. The appearance of complexity is one of the things that allowed the banks to keep doing what was getting them (and us) into trouble for as long as they did. Some of their more arcane practices were apparently beyond the grasp even of the regulators.

But there's one man who manages to cut through the fog of complexity and obfuscation with a laser-beam of clarity. Warren Buffett was the world's richest man until his chum Bill Gates knocked him off the perch. Even so, he remains the world's most successful investor. Previously known as 'the sage of Omaha', he is now revered as the 'oracle of Omaha', so good is his investment record.

But prodigious wealth, and a fondness for bridge, is where the similarity between the two men ends. Gates, the über-nerd, controls a vast and glossy empire from Microsoft's sculpted headquarters outside Seattle. Buffett, the hayseed from the heart of the Midwest, makes his decisions from Berkshire Hathaway's scruffy office in downtown Omaha, Nebraska.

Buffett doesn't buy fashionable companies, only those that he deems to be well managed. He has never bought a technology stock because he doesn't understand the business. He owns a modest suburban house and drives a second-hand car. His company website looks like a first-year design project, while the Berkshire Hathaway AGM has all the sophistication of a country fayre, where 30,000 adoring shareholders come to eat ice cream, drink cherry coke and sit at the feet of their guru.

For all the homespun veneer, Buffett is in his own way probably just as much of a nerd as Gates — undoubtedly brilliant, maybe a little autistic, certainly obsessive-compulsive. But there's one thing he has mastered, which is plain speaking (in marked contrast to his bridge partner's organisation which, as you've already pointed out elsewhere in this book, John, is a world-class purveyor of technobabble).

In 1998, such is Buffett's standing in the investment world, he was invited to write a preface to the US Securities and Exchange Commission's Plain English Handbook. He concluded with this 'one unoriginal but useful tip':

Write with a specific person in mind. When writing Berkshire Hathaway's annual report, I pretend that I'm talking to my sisters. I have no trouble picturing them: Though highly intelligent, they are not experts in accounting or finance. They will understand plain English, but jargon may puzzle them. My goal is simply to give them the information I would wish them to supply me if our positions were reversed. To succeed, I don't need to be Shakespeare; I must, though, have a sincere desire to inform. No siblings to write to? Borrow mine: Just begin with 'Dear Doris and Bertie.'

For that alone he gets my vote. If you have a moment, try googling 'Warren Buffett's Letters to Berkshire Hathaway Shareholders', especially the letter for 2008, when the recession started to bite. There's nothing else out there like them.

80 THINGS TO DO

Take the oracle's advice. Think about what having 'a sincere desire to inform' really means: telling your reader what you want to say or what they want to know (by no means always the same thing)? And as you write, picture someone 'highly intelligent though not expert [in your field].' What would you want to know if you were in their position?

Week 22
John to Jamie

TO BE CLEAR

I've just been reading Michael Lewis' book, *The Big Short*, which is a good read about the origins of the world's financial crisis. Here are a couple of quotations from it:

Bond market terminology was designed less to convey meaning than to bewilder outsiders.

When Charlie asked Deutsche Bank exactly what assets secured an asset-backed security, he was handed lists of abbreviations and more acronyms — RMBS, HELs, HELOCs, Alt-A — along with categories of credit he did not know existed.

So some business people have a vested interest in being unclear. It's in their interest but not in ours. From these examples we could argue that it was the deliberately obscure use of language that brought about the financial crash we're now suffering.

No wonder then that 'clarity' is valued. I'd wager 'clarity' would come top in any survey trying to answer the question, what's the most important quality in business writing? Which makes me think...

Clarity is an essential quality for so much communication. But I always want more. Clear communication does a job but the job is limited. We don't necessarily want our words to do exactly what it says on the tin. Because words can reach deeper inside us, can find emotions and express them with personality, make a persuasive case that leads us to do something. The benefits of purely rational clarity can leave you wanting more.

It was interesting this week when I was doing some one-to-one coaching at The Writer for a client from the professional services world. There's a sector that places an apparently high value on 'clarity', even if it consistently obscures clarity with jargon, acronyms and abstract nouns. I asked my client to write something about the God of Clarity. She responded brilliantly by writing a piece titled, 'The God of Clarity is called Sunshine'. Sunshine throws light on objects that are obscured, removing darkness when you can't see to the essence of what you want to convey.

This made me feel much more positive about clarity. It's a good example of the power of metaphor, reaching deep to a source of inner honesty. It makes clear, too, that there is rational *and* emotional clarity. Often, it's emotional clarity — perhaps achieved by metaphor — that really shines a light on difficult meaning. As writers we need to have an honest desire to be as clear as possible — because clarity, at its best, is close to honesty.

79 THINGS TO DO

Who is the God of Clarity? Write the story of this god from your own viewpoint, imagining the god in your own working situation. What does he do? How does he do it? Who are his enemies?

Jamie to John

AN HONEST TALE

Yes, I would say they were siblings, if not even twins. I'm not sure it's possible to be clear — in the rational *and* emotional sense, as you say — about something that's fundamentally untrue or dishonest. Yet it's a sad fact of modern business life that competing pressures and responsibilities — to shareholders, employees, partners, the media, the bottom line — see honesty and truth being sacrificed daily on the altar of expediency. That's not to imply that people set out actively to deceive (at least, not most), but that usually it's just too damned difficult to give the whole, unvarnished truth. Alan Clark's famous words, 'being economical with the actualité' spring to mind.

This is where stories become so important — we keep coming back to them, don't we? Your client hit on a truth when she wrote, 'The God of Clarity is called Sunshine'. It was *her* truth, not *the* truth, but it was still unarguable and we know at once what she meant. It's clear because we can understand it quickly and easily. It's honest because it comes from that authentic, inner place you describe — her heart, you could say. And it's truthful because it says something universal. We can't judge it, it simply is. And that's its power. It leaves us room to attach our own thoughts and feelings to it.

In the task you ask people to identify the enemy, the being or beings that obstruct the god in question. Knowing who the god is up against helps us to understand their purpose more clearly. The God of Honesty has many enemies and Dishonesty, also called Deceit, is only one of them. There's Insincerity, Boastfulness, Fear, Reticence, Indifference… the list goes on. What's more, they're all characters that make regular appearances in business writing; even, I'm afraid to say, in business storytelling — or the case study, as it's most commonly known.

The trouble with case studies is that they're dull and smug, and they tell us what to think and feel. They start, for example, by describing what the client needed and move swiftly to conclude that we helped that client brilliantly. Yet we don't read stories for victory, we read them for adversity — and there's certainly no shortage of that in business. So there's an opportunity to tell honest stories that really resonate. Stories that have emotional depth because they talk about real people rather than projects or initiatives, and real difficulties rather than vague 'challenges', those watered-down abstractions that scarcely sully the path to corporate success.

I've always liked the following story. The McIlhenny Company of Louisiana is on the skids. Tabasco sales have fallen year on year and the directors are holding a crisis meeting. Enter the tea-boy with his trolley. He sees the grim faces, the plunging graph, and asks what they're talking about. Priding themselves on their southern openness, they tell him. I know what to do, he says after a moment. Tell us, they humour him. Easy, he replies, make the hole bigger. And they do.

It's a simple story and it doesn't set out to make a point. It doesn't argue, though we draw our own conclusions from it about the value of honesty and openness. But it does tell of human struggle, of emotions like worry and relief; and so it should, because business life doesn't just echo human experience, it *is* human experience. 'Stories do not argue,' says my friend, the Edinburgh storyteller, David Campbell. 'They speak to the heart. They are emissaries and luminaries in which we find … snatches of our shared human journey.' Surely that makes them the handmaidens of honesty.

78 THINGS TO DO
Now write the story of the god of your own
business specialisation. Perhaps it's marketing or

communications or brand management... Again, who are its enemies? Then step back into the real world and see what stories you can find within your organisation that say something honest and meaningful about what your part of the business does.

Week 23
John to Jamie

WINNING STORIES

When I was working for a brand consultancy we might have substituted the word 'brand' for 'story'. Story seems to me much more compelling and universal. And brand consultancies now routinely use the word 'story' to describe what they do, even though they are not necessarily good storytellers.

'Brand' now means much more than it used to do. It used to be confined mainly to consumer goods that you find on shop shelves, whereas now corporations, celebrities and even events think of themselves as brands. Each of them needs to have a story. And what that story needs to express is a clear sense of purpose.

Is this the difference between the stories that win Olympic bids, and those that don't? When London won the bid for the 2012 Olympics, the consensus was that London had created a good narrative about the past linking to the future. It had begun to tell that through Seb Coe's personal story of his own childhood experiences of watching the Games and being inspired to become an athlete. This aspirational story was reinforced in every word and image that followed.

The man behind the winning campaign, Mike Lee, commented:

Great campaigns are built on great narratives. Everything you do has to fit in with that narrative.

Four years later he helped Rio de Janeiro win the 2016 Olympics, making the point:

As the London team did, Rio had to combine the rational and the emotional, building a story that understood the context of the Olympic movement.

For brands, stories can express powerfully what they are really here for. My client in one of Australia's biggest financial institutions put it like this: 'What gets us up in the morning?' Apart that is from the expected purpose of a bank, to make money. Is there a deeper, more human purpose? The people in the bank believed so and asked me to write stories that would express it.

The telling of factual stories — ranging from the conventional building of businesses through fulfilment of personal aspirations and to support of aboriginal art — led to the creation of stories in many fictional genres. So I wrote the opening pages of stories in different genres — fantasy, fairy tale, Dan Brown, detective, chick lit and Manga. It gave people a different way of understanding their organisation's purpose — and a better way than the conventional, formulaic description of a brand's mission, vision and values.

77 THINGS TO DO

Think of a brand you know well. What is its purpose? What gets its people up in the morning, choosing to work there? Write the opening page of a story in a genre of your choice, in a way that will make clear the brand's purpose.

HEAD, HEART AND VOICE

Such is the power of stories that sometimes it's just the vestige of one, the trace of it still hanging in the air, that serves to give a brand that depth and connection with its customers. It's hard to think of anything else in business that can persuade in this almost homeopathic way.

I read some time ago that in Denmark, eggs from free-range hens had conquered over half the market despite the fact that they not only cost 20% more than non-free-range eggs, but also their quality was not 20% better than other eggs. So what were people increasingly willing to pay extra for? A story. In this case, the story of the hen that is free to scratch the earth and see the sky. No one had told egg buyers this story, no campaign had been built around it; but it was implicit in the idea of the free-range hen. People had told the story to themselves.

I found myself in a John Lewis department store the other day. There are two things most people know about this British retail landmark. One is its famous slogan, 'Never knowingly undersold', with the accompanying pledge to refund the difference if you find the same item cheaper elsewhere. The other is the fact that it's a partnership, effectively owned by its employees.

Do many of John Lewis's customers know the story of how the partnership came about? I would be very surprised. Perhaps some people have the vague notion of a philanthropic founder — which is almost right, it was his son — but it doesn't matter. The important thing is that the idea of a partnership is itself a story and a compelling one at that, perhaps because it's all too unusual in the modern business world. In any case, it's a story of fairness and democracy and collaboration — and we like that. As soon as we know it, the idea of shopping at John Lewis acquires a resonance that goes way beyond the rational.

When that story is reinforced with language that embodies the same values, the effect is irresistible. 'At John Lewis we don't just define value by price,' they say. 'Though our prices are some of the most competitive on the high street, we also offer incredible value in the quality of our products, as well as our expert, highly professional service.'

The thing is, it's all true. And we believe it partly because the experience of shopping in the store confirms it; partly because it chimes with everything we know about the ethos of the business (whose 67,000 partners/employees received a bonus for 2007/8 worth 20% of their gross salaries); partly because the way they say it is simple, direct and, above all, honest. The John Lewis Partnership is a brand whose voice is truly in harmony with its head and its heart. That makes for very powerful communication.

76 THINGS TO DO

Think of some of the products we take for granted in our lives — bread for example. What stories does it suggest to you? What are the emotions you associate with it? Now imagine you have to write a brochure for a generic brand organisation, let's call it the Bread Board. What's the tone of voice you would use for bread?

Week 24

John to Jamie

SMALL CRAFT WARNINGS

You're right about the 'traces' of a story. To a large extent a brand's story is beyond the control of the brand owner.

That's no bad thing, but any brand owner will want to have some control over its own brand story. The way you tell it matters. You need to tell the brand's story with respect for your own craft as a writer rather than as a way to agree on a collection of buzz words. I often think that business writing is really a form of translation. We translate one impenetrable form of English into a different, more understandable and more engaging form.

As with any language, you get better at it as you practice more, and this is a matter of craft. I'm just reading a book by Richard Sennett called *The Craftsman*. He argues that we are in danger of losing craft skills, and that the way we have always learnt crafts — by practice, trial, error, learning from mistakes — is being lost. An architect, for example, can now produce computer-aided designs to give you, on a screen, a real sense of a designed space. But what is lost is the process of really understanding that space by going through the development of designs that comes with repeating and revising drawings. The architect inhabits the space less, the machine does the living and learning instead. And, perhaps, you end up with unlivable spaces.

The same danger faces us as writers. We need to keep developing our craft, to avoid sinking back into easy, time-saving ways of working. For myself, I always write first drafts (and often second ones) in pencil on paper. It puts you more in touch with your thinking.

The Sennett book was recommended by my client at an engineering firm called Max Fordham. As a non-engineer she's trying successfully to understand the ethos of the company where the engineers would much rather *do* the job than spend time writing about it. She asked me to meet the engineers, find out more about what they do and how they go about their jobs, then produce some descriptive words to sum them up. I wrote this:

> *We're engineers. We work closely with architects to design buildings that really work. This means we're concerned with the big picture and the small detail of buildings.*
>
> *In a traditional sense we are building services engineers. But our approach is broad as well as specific. We engineer air, light, sound and energy. In doing so we cross boundaries between engineering disciplines, because that breadth of vision achieves the best buildings for our clients. We're whole building engineers.*

I enjoyed talking to the engineers. What we shared was a sense of craft. We agreed on these words that can be spoken in a minute but took weeks to write.

75 THINGS TO DO

Set aside an hour to write a paragraph that describes an activity you do — a hobby, perhaps, or a sport — something that is familiar and helps define you because it is so much a part of your everyday thinking. Now write paragraphs to introduce that activity to people who might not understand it. Write at least 10 different versions. Compare them. Edit to get to one version that you feel expresses the activity best.

Jamie to John

SELF ASSEMBLY

I seem to have the theme of 'traces' in my head at the moment. And the thing about craft is that it leaves a trace of the craftsman's presence in whatever they have created. The 'personality' of anything made, in any sense — physical or conceptual — by one person derives directly from the care and effort, the skill and commitment with which they made it.

In the physical world, the opposite of craft is mass production. It's the difference between a table made by a cabinet-maker and a table you can buy at IKEA. The crafted table bears the maker's personal stamp in the choice of wood, the shape, the proportions and the finish. And the personality is present not just in the design. The maker's hands have been on it, their effort and sweat has gone into it. They leave something of themselves behind in it.

The IKEA table, however pleasant it may look, has no intrinsic personality. Yes, it has been designed, its form has sprung from someone's imagination, but thereafter human hands have been absent. It has been made by machines controlled by computers. It's functional, bland, homogenous and ultimately dull because it has no real character.

The analogy with writing is obvious. Although we haven't yet got to the point where writing can be automated, businesses, as we keep saying, too often write like automata; or rather, people who write for businesses too often use language that's functional, bland, homogenous and dull. It's simpler to choose the mass-produced phrase over the crafted phrase. And if this book's about anything it's about the importance of writing as a craft.

Paradoxically, perhaps, IKEA themselves understand this. There's evidence of craft in the way they use words (not always in their assembly instructions, admittedly), but certainly on their website. This is from their founding story:

> *At the age of five Ingvar Kamprad starts selling matches to his nearby neighbours and by the time he is seven, he starts selling further afield, using his bicycle. He finds that he can buy matches in bulk cheaply in Stockholm and re-sell them individually at a very low price but still make a good profit. From matches he expands to selling flower seeds, greeting cards, Christmas tree decorations, and later pencils and ballpoint pens.*

In the first place, the language sounds like a literal translation from Swedish. This may be deliberate, it may not be. Either way, I find it rather endearing. But there's also a clear desire to tell a story here, and to tell it in a tone of voice which may be typically Swedish but which also echoes the matter-of-fact, no-nonsense character of IKEA's products. There's thought behind this. Care and effort has gone into choosing the words to tell the story in a particular way. Their goods may be mass-produced but that doesn't mean they can't be proud of them, and proud of the great business story that goes with them.

Finding the most engaging way to tell the world about themselves, as you did with your engineers, John, imbuing the words with personality, even if it's only a trace — that's craft.

74 THINGS TO DO

What does the word 'craft' mean to you? Take a clean sheet of paper and write for five minutes without lifting your hand from the page, starting with the words, 'The craft of writing is …' Let your thoughts go wherever they take you. Write whatever comes out. Above all, don't stop to think, just keep writing!

Week 25
John to Jamie

AND A WORD ABOUT GRAMMAR

We need to think of grammar as part of our craft, although our hearts don't lift up at the thought. People worry about grammar — we see it all the time in our workshops. I confess that most of my understanding of English grammar comes from having studied Latin at school. It still remains my best help when analysing the parts of a sentence, understanding the relationship between subject and object, the different tenses, the passive or active form of a verb. In Latin, an inflected language, such things are clearer, you see the structure in the way word endings change. In English we don't have such help. Does it matter?

Strangely I received this e-mail today:

Hi mate,
This is jenilia

We do provide a unique article on your topics suggested relevant on your interest at no cost. No duplication or copying of the article

is done. we right contents exclusively for your site on demand.
We also give Copy rights for articles to your site on security base.

Articles which we providing
* Will be unique.
* Will not be redistributed to other sites.
* You will own the entire copyrights.

I've no idea who 'jenilia' is, addressing me as 'mate' but forgetting to give a capital letter to his or her name. Apparently he's offering to help with me with my writing, which seems a kind offer but one I declined in my mind in the first line or two of his e-mail. My decision was taken because his poor grammar, spelling and vocabulary influenced me. So grammar does matter if it gives a negative impression.

Soon afterwards, I received this e-mail:

Free guide to gaining efficiency through HR technology

The role of HR within modern business has faced numerous changes, and the role of HR software has had to evolve to meet new demands. The right HR software allows you complete visibility across your entire organisation and the accurate and timely information you acquire enables you to improve employee return on investment. This guide offers advice to senior HR professionals when choosing the latest HRIS (Human Resource Information System), identifying the key functionality you need and, most importantly, how to command stakeholder interest if your organisation has outgrown its existing system.

This is a more typical example of sales material for business. In terms of grammar, it's much better than jenilia's e-mail, but it leaves me even more resistant to its message. It's so deadly dull and unappealing. So writing grammatically will not in itself achieve all you wish.

My only conclusion is that it's part of our craft to try to write with decent grammar. At the same time we need to realise that there are no 'rules' of grammar in English, there are only conventions that we follow. And those conventions evolve over time as idioms change. But such signs of life are to be welcomed. So please let's not get hung up with 'rules' remembered from schooldays, like you should never start sentences with 'And' or 'But'. My most frequent response to that old shibboleth, to use an interesting Biblical word, is to ask people to look at the first chapter of the Book of Genesis. Count the number of sentences beginning with 'And'. The answer is 32 of the 34 sentences in the Authorised version.

You could argue that 'And' is taken to excess in that example. Perhaps the notion of excess is our clearest guide in matters of grammar. Sentences that are too long, too dense; words that are too long, too obscure. TOO MANY CAPITALS WORK AGAINST UNDERSTANDING: the US Federal highway administration decided to change 250,000 street signs in New York city because research showed that excessive use of capitals was dangerous. The same surely applies to exclamation marks!! Think carefully, frequently and often about the excessive use of adverbs (though it would be truly silly to ban them altogether). And remember too that not every adverb ends in '-ly'.

73 THINGS TO DO

Rewrite the HR paragraph shown above by changing as many of the nouns into verbs as you can. Assess what happens as a result. Is it much clearer?

Jamie to John

LINGERING SUPERSTITIONS

I can't resist the temptation to quote Sir Ernest Gowers on what we used to be told was that most heinous of grammatical crimes, the split infinitive. Gowers was a civil servant who is best known for his style guides on written English, and in particular his 1965 revision of *Fowler's Modern English Usage*. This is what he said:

> *The English-speaking world may be divided into (1) those who neither know nor care what a split infinitive is; (2) those who do not know but care very much; (3) those who know and condemn; (4) those who know and approve; and (5) those who know and distinguish. Those who neither know nor care are the vast majority, and are a happy folk, to be envied by most of the minority classes...*

Gowers himself was an absolute master of clarity and style. He also had a wicked sense of humour. On the split infinitive — 'to really understand' as opposed to 'really to understand', for example — he concludes that the correct usage is largely a matter of personal taste, based on whether it sounds all right and doesn't interfere with the sense. As for 'And' beginning sentences, he makes this often-quoted observation:

> *That it is a solecism to beginning a sentence with and is a faintly lingering superstition.*

Gowers obviously relished the English language, understood it profoundly, and loved having fun using it. He also tended to the common sense view of things, recognizing that people trapped by dimly remembered rules were largely missing the point. In most cases, those 'who know and distinguish' got his vote. In effect he was saying that as long as you understand the basic principles, you can rely on your ear to do much of the work.

Which brings me to the importance of reading what you have written aloud. If you have the luxury of your own private working space, you should always speak your words aloud to yourself. I do, every day, every single word I write. If you share an office and are worried about looking (or sounding) slightly mad, speak them aloud in your head. Try it. It's perfectly possible. (To digress for a moment, close your mouth, let your tongue rest against your lower teeth. Now think a thought, any thought. At the same time, note what happens in your tongue. That gives you an idea of how closely linked are the thought and the word.)

But back to reading aloud … it may seem terribly obvious, but hearing yourself speaking what you've written gives you so many clues as to whether it will read well. Are you running out of breath? Then your sentences are too long. Is it monotonous? You need to vary the sentence length. Does it sound flat? You've probably got too many abstract nouns and not enough verbs.

Punctuation was originally devised for actors, to indicate in the text where they should take a breath. It was practical, not something invented by some sadistic grammarian to bedevil generations of schoolchildren. So were most of the 'rules' of grammar. They were practical guidelines, designed to help us use this extraordinarily rich, versatile language that is English to the best possible effect — to make the best sense. And what communicator doesn't want to do that?

72 THINGS TO DO

Take something you've written to be read, not heard, and try reading it aloud as if it were a speech. Would it hold an audience? If the answer is no, why should you expect it to hold a reader? The more it sounds like a speech, the more likely it is to have energy, pace and rhythm and the more engaging it'll be.

IN BRIEF

'To boldly go' might be the most widely used split infinitive of our lifetime. Captain Kirk in Star Trek is not necessarily the best linguistic guide but the phrase works. It works particularly when, as you suggest, you listen to it (probably in the voice of William Shatner). The spoken words convey a greater sense of mission and adventure than the slightly hesitant cadence of an alternative like 'to go boldly'.

'Boldly going' is a good idea for any writer to embrace as a brief. So often we're given timorous briefs that discourage any thoughts of boldness, but as writers we depend on the quality of the briefs we're given. I don't mean that a brief should try to cover every angle; indeed, the best briefs are those that are bold enough to encourage possibilities that the briefer might not have imagined.

A few years ago I was called in by Unilever to help them write better briefs. Unilever produced briefs that went into great detail about target audiences and demographics, gave reams of back-up information and research, but lost the essential point: 'What's our purpose here?' The resulting advertising, in response to those briefs, disappointed the Unilever team — all bright marketers. The ads ticked the boxes in response to the brief but lacked vitality. What was going wrong?

I ran a workshop for the team, sending them back to their own briefs, exploring creative ideas inside people's heads and asking them to write some pieces that seemed unrelated to their brief. The penny dropped that you cannot channel creativity safely through a brief that tries to anticipate every risk. Be prepared to encourage risks and, more often than not, you'll be rewarded with a more interesting response. Being clear about the purpose you want to achieve is the best guide.

People enjoyed writing. They 'got it'. Then they thought of the briefing forms they would need to fill in the next time they briefed the ad agency — all those boxes, fields to be filled, supplementary information to be supplied. 'What about the template?' a brave soul asked. It was a question that had to be faced.

The marketing director was an exuberant Brazilian woman. She heard the question, her eyes flashed and her hands thumped down on the table. 'The template is us!' she exclaimed dramatically.

I think that's true. Sometimes it's not the brief that holds us back, it's ourselves. So ask for the brief, question it and explore it, create your own if one is not forthcoming. If you're given a brief of almost impossible tightness, welcome it; this might spark the best work you've ever done.

71 THINGS TO DO

Take a recent brief that you've been given. What do you like about it? What's helpful or unhelpful? What was missing that might actually have helped you write your words more effectively? Rewrite the brief and show it to your client, explaining what you've done. This might be the last time you work for that client ('boldly go') — or it might be the start of a much better partnership.

Jamie to John

ORAL HISTORY

'Boldly go' is not just a good motto for following a brief. It's a useful exhortation to anyone trying to break free of the monotony of business speak. I use it all the time in workshops. I ask people to re-write a piece of the usual dull, self-congratulatory corporate text in a style that's closer to the way they would speak it. 'Go beyond your comfort zone,' I tell them. 'Make it sound *really* informal, as if you were talking to a friend who knows nothing about your work.'

Brows furrow and pencils tremble in hands (so strong is the conditioning, so quickly does our language become institutionalised). Then they read out what they've written — and guess what? It sounds perfectly normal. It doesn't come across as being 'dumbed down'. It's not slangy or over-familiar. And usually it's much easer to understand.

So how did we get here? How did we reach the point where we have one language for work and another for the rest of our lives? In one we tend to engage with all the unique characteristics and faculties that make us the individuals we are. In the other — only really half a language — we leave a large part of our personalities behind. Cipher is a frightening and demeaning word, but to some extent it's what modern business-speak makes us.

Fear, of course, has a lot to answer for. Fear of looking stupid or out of touch, fear of being called to account, fear of losing control or authority. The less of ourselves we reveal the more we distance ourselves from the possible consequences of what we say or write.

But how did it come to this? I believe modern business language has been brewing for at least 250 years — though some people would probably say much longer. It certainly comes to us via the age of reason and early scientific enquiry, when objectivity was the watchword; it comes via the subsequent industrial revolution, when new technical processes were the dominant force; the expansion of trade and empire, from which a new vocabulary of commerce emerged; Victorian paternalism and love of litigation, which saw the full flowering of legalese; the periods of austerity following two world wars, and the language of twentieth century military command (in particular from Vietnam, the first televised war), with its talk of campaigns and strategic objectives; the IT revolution with a whole new almost mandatory technological dialect; and the explosive growth of management consultancy and the MBA culture — quasi-academic, pseudo-scientific.

Add to all that the most recent and baneful influence, the culture of measurement, and the resulting cocktail is scarcely a language at all since at its worst it fails to communicate on almost any human level — which of course is why, as Orwell's *Nineteen Eighty-Four* so brilliantly illustrated, it suits some people's purposes perfectly.

It is also why writers have such an enormous job educating the business world. The task is not just to help people find a simpler language; it's to show them that the openness and honesty that must underpin this language are not just better precepts for good communication than disingenuity and obfuscation, but that they open the doors to creativity and imagination and personality — all those characteristics that language totalitarians seek to suppress. That does take a certain boldness, you and I would be the first to admit. It doesn't always win friends. But as so many of the examples in this book should already have demonstrated, the evidence that it works is pretty overwhelming.

70 THINGS TO DO

Take a typical piece of business writing and rewrite it as if you were explaining it to an elderly relative who has no knowledge of the subject. Be bold. Be conversational. Use everyday expressions. Say 'I' and 'we', 'didn't' and 'couldn't'. How would it sound coming from the chief executive of that business?

Part 3

SUMMER

John to Jamie

THE MYTH OF OBJECTIVITY

Summer has come and we're in the South of France on a Dark Angels writing retreat. We're with a good bunch of people, all writers for business, taking a week away from one genre to explore another. Instead of writing policy papers, they'll write novels, stories, poetry — at least for a week. Perhaps it's the sunshine, or good company, French food and wine, or just being somewhere else, but this retreat makes it easier to connect with a style of writing that's joyfully subjective. What a relief. So I'm finishing my novella, *The Angel of the Stories,* which is about as far away as you can get from the joyless objectivity many institutions see as the purpose of writing.

You wrote last week, Jamie, about the various historical influences that have brought us to the current state of business writing. You listed the industrial revolution, Victorian legalese, 20th century military command and the MBA culture, among others. All interesting and plausible reasons for the state we're in.

One other reason occurs to me. It's the pretence of objectivity demanded by a variety of institutions: the academic world, civil service, local government, corporate governance. The charade that it's professional to rely on facts not emotions, that it's best not to write a strong opinion.

I ran a workshop last week at The Writer, where we looked at a piece of 'professional' writing containing this phrase: 'We are not unconvinced by…' It's the language of one professional not wanting to criticise another but expecting you to read between the lines. A professional game is being played, in this case by CABE (Commission on Architecture and the Built Environment) writing to a distinguished architect. Such language appears in the review paper, meeting minutes or annual report. It's *Yes, Minister*'s Sir Humphrey writing to his superior with a knowing smile.

In the same workshop I asked people to write a short piece about something they felt strongly about, to show an opinion.

Automatically the language changed from that of the academic/ managerial cult of objectivity. Language fell naturally towards personal pronouns, active verbs, short words, strong rhythms, alliteration, verbal games. The language of emotion: convincing, persuasive, engaging.

The managerial world often tries to avoid that kind of emotive language because managers find it hard to manage people's emotions. Actually, they find it hard to manage people — it's much easier to manage a machine. The machine does what you tell it to do. So the corporation prefers to speak to you as if you're a machine — in the style of the Dicken's character, Gradgrind, educating you with that narrow, unsustaining diet of 'facts, facts, facts'.

It's no way to communicate. We can go in one direction or another at work, it's up to you as the manager or the managed. But it's your choice of words that sets out the way you're going. It's all part of a lifelong education, which has to be built on encouraging people to be creative. A good place to take encouragement is by watching Sir Ken Robinson's TED talk 'Schools kill creativity'.

69 THINGS TO DO

Watch the TED talk, 'Schools kill creativity', by Sir Ken Robinson. It is a brilliant 20 minutes of thought-provoking communication. Then write for 20 minutes with your own thoughts inspired by that talk. File those words away. Let them brew. They'll emerge in something that you write over the next year.

Jamie to John

WHO DARES WINS

Sir Ken Robinson is not just a brilliant communicator. He's a bold one. He dares to challenge the conventional wisdom about the way we educate ourselves (in which, incidentally, the perceived needs of the business world play their part). He does it with passion and humour as well as with fact and reason. When we watch him we know that we're getting all of him — head, heart and soul — which is why what he says is so compelling.

Looking at the faces and postures of our companions on the retreat here, I have no doubt that they, too, are putting all of themselves into what they say. In shady nooks on the terraces, down beside the pool or in cool corners of the house, bent over laptops or notebooks, each individual is a study in absorption. For this week at least they are free to write from the very core of their beings, from the creative source we all contain within us, if only we can tap into it.

As I wrestle with my own project — the last in a series of three novels for teenagers — I think of the other writers I will spend time with in Edinburgh later this summer at the International Book Festival. Some are my good friends. Some are acquaintances, to be caught up with once a year. Some are my heroes — literary giants whose mere presence reduces me to a state of tongue-tied awe. And some are those whose work intrigues me and whose events I feel bold enough to chair.

This year, the latter group includes four household names — William Dalrymple, Roddy Doyle, Melvyn Bragg and Alexander McCall Smith, and three less widely known but no less interesting writers — the veteran Scottish novelist Allan Massie, the *Observer's* deputy editor Robert McCrum, and the linguistics professor David Crystal (whom I've already mentioned elsewhere in this book).

Why did I choose these seven? It's hard to say. Their subject matter ranges from Indian mysticism to the Irish Troubles; the South Bank Show to Precious Ramotswe and the Ladies' No 1 Detective Agency; the Royal Stuart dynasty to the King James Bible and a globalised version of the English language. Doubtless there are sub-conscious connections there, which I'm not about to explore here.

They have one obvious thing in common, though. They are people who inspire because they do not stand apart from themselves. To read their work or hear them speak is to receive the whole of them, not some filtered version where their real personalities have been subordinated to the needs of the narrow interest group they serve, their language reined in by the processes and formulations of their professions. They know how to stand on the hilltop where they can see widely, and communicate their vision in simple but well-chosen words. They're not afraid to employ imagery, metaphor, humour — all the tools we use daily to communicate with one another as emotionally functional human beings.

In short, they dare to reveal themselves as they truly are, and in doing so they release that energy which, as Sir Ken Robinson so compellingly argues, is what we call creativity. This is what gives their ideas the power to influence us, their readers or audiences. In that respect are they really so different from the business managers who use language to influence *their* readers or audiences?

68 THINGS TO DO

Have you ever stopped to think what creativity really means to you as a writer? Try writing for 10 minutes, starting with 'I'm creative when…' Then write for another 10 minutes, starting with the words 'The things that get in the way…'.

Week 28
John to Jamie

THE JOY OF WRITING

'No tears in the writer, no tears in the reader.' It's something I've heard you say in workshops. But the tears can be tears of joy, because it seems to me there's no point in writing unless it gives the writer pleasure. Even if that pleasure can be a masochistic one, a sense of exquisite agony as you struggle to reach a point of satisfaction — at least enough to let go of what you've written.

How often, though, can you experience joy from writing for business? Perhaps not often enough, though I think instantly of stories I've written for Guinness, packaging copy for Budgens, a brochure for Ila Spa, even a calendar (one of my first writing jobs) for the National Economic Development Office. But I believe it's important to seek out the possibilities for joyful writing. If you accept that your business writing is going to be functional and joyless (does what it says on the tin), you'll restrict your own potential to do more with your writing.

For me, this is where 26 plays a particular role. Through this writers' group, set up primarily for business writers who want to champion and improve their craft, I've initiated and contributed to many projects. The results of the latest, '26 Treasures', are now arriving in my e-mail inbox and will then appear on the '26 Treasures' website. What really strikes me about these pieces of exactly 62 words about an object in the V&A is the evident joy that people get from writing.

We've a wonderful spectrum of writers, ranging from the most respected poets to seasoned business writers to novelists to young writers still trying to find their voices in the world of words. But I'm sure each of them recognises the sense of joy experienced through crafting their words to fit the exact number of 62.

It's what keeps us going, constantly returning to the need to put down the right words in the right order in a way that is individual and distinctive. Whether it's former poet laureate Sir Andrew Motion almost whooping 'roll over John Keats' when told he'd been paired with the bust of Homer; or tyro writer Beth Norris just thrilled by the prospect of seeing her words made public. We recognise the emotion. Beth wrote to me: 'My old Nan did a dance around the living room!'

It's all too easy to get blasé. We need to keep fresh the joy of writing and being read.

Go to www.26treasures.com and dip into the various pieces dealing with objects. Look at the variety of approaches possible in response to the same brief. Here are the pieces that Jamie and I wrote — mine was about an 18ᵗʰ century Rococo candle stand, Jamie's about a 17ᵗʰ century document case. Choose an object from your own life that is precious to you. Write about it in exactly 62 words.

Still standing
Once I said
I've seen
the light
my little joke, oh

so rococo

but those days
are gone
while I stand
somewhatsquatly
dustycornerishly
deprived of light.
Gaze who will.
When once I lit up soirées,
dinners, balls,
my dolphins winking at
the daily dalliances,
now I've come to rest
beneath unenquiring eyes.
You can call it a living but not a life.

Pro posteri

They come here
With the glance of his blade
Still searing their shoulders
I leather apron'd
They in silks and brocades
Flushed, clasping letters patent
'Make me a box,' they say,
'That my children's children's children
May cherish my ennoblement.
Make it to last.'
I finger my chisel
Picturing pine, brass, tooled morocco
And smiling say
'That I surely will, my Lord.'

Jamie to John

HEARING VOICES

The starting point for almost everything I write is a voice. Even before I know what I'm going to say I need to have an idea of how it is going to sound, a sense of the personality that is going to come through the words.

When I'm writing fiction it may just be a phrase I keep hearing that becomes the basis for a character. With other writing, I find the clues where I can. At the V&A, standing in front of my object, a document case, I wondered for a moment whether the voice I would hear might be that of the owner, or the object itself, but the one I very quickly and clearly heard was, in fact, that of its maker.

Which is all very well for novels and poems, but what about business documents? Of course, many businesses these days have clearly defined tones of voice, but many more don't. Where, then, does one find the distinct voice that gives an organisation its personality?

Here is a case in point, one of the more challenging of my career. I've recently completed a document for a community of Benedictine monks that makes public their need for support. They want money for their buildings and for their work as teachers, priests and missionaries. They also badly need fresh blood; their population is ageing and new vocations come few and far between in this secular age.

But how do monks sound in the 21st century? How *should* they sound? Certainly not pious — that would antagonise people. Not even overly religious — that's their internal business, their process and procedure. But spiritual, most definitely. Compassionate? Yes. And contemporary? A little, perhaps, but timeless would be better.

I grappled with the voice for a long time and in the end — as always — it was the research that gave me what I needed. From reading and re-reading the notes of my visit something eventually emerged that seemed to sound right:

> *Each day, in the words we recite, the chants we sing, the cycle of prayer we observe, we repeat the instructions set down by St. Benedict in the sixth century. This is the deep and enduring pulse that regulates our lives. In all that time, even in the darkest moments of our history, it has never wavered.*

Research is the process by which we experience the warp and weft of a particular universe, even if we can't personally experience its spiritual or emotional underpinnings. As a non-religious person I can't share the monks' faith any more than, as a non-entrepreneur, I can share a businessman's conviction for his particular business. But I can at least make an imaginative connection with that very human quality of belief.

So the sunlight on the monastery lawns, the simplicity and majesty of the church, the fine old faces of the silent monks at their meals, the contemplative calm of the cloisters, the gentle conversations about monastic life in the 21st century, all fed into something which, through the action of imagination, became a form of empathy or understanding, if not actually a shared belief.

That's where the voice came from. And for me — returning to your point about joy, John — the joy was first in hearing it and then in having the monks confirm that what I had heard was true.

66 THINGS TO DO

Now that you've written 62 words about your own precious object, give yourself a further 10 or 15 minutes to write a monologue from the perspective of the object. Give it a voice. What does it say to you?

Week 29
John to Jamie

THE PATTERNS OF LIFE

I think we both research in similar ways. It's not facts or hard information we're after, but clues. We listen, we look, we use our senses. What we're really after is a pattern, a sense that what someone said in one place fits with something you saw in another place.

Last week I was having lunch with a former client (now friend) called David Croom. When David was MD of book publishers Routledge in the 1990s, I led the Newell and Sorrell team that created the Routledge identity. The most distinctive feature of the identity was the use of pattern — adapted from a book of Islamic art that David showed us. The thought fitted, and it came together with words and visuals to make a successful identity.

This conversation reminded me that, when I visited the Alhambra in Granada and the Mezquita in Cordoba last year, they appealed to me particularly because of their beautiful use of pattern. Why did the Arabic peoples come up with all these patterns? There is a strong strain of Islamic thinking, not necessarily endorsed by the Quran, that images of people and life should not be created and displayed. This does not apply in every Islamic culture, but certainly there aren't any pictures of people or animals in the Alhambra. Instead, there are many beautiful graphic patterns.

This interested me afresh because, of course, it's another example of constraints leading to creativity. Denied the opportunity to paint representational pictures, Islamic artists came up with patterns — rather beautiful ones.

It's harder to see patterns in writing in quite the same visual way. But as readers and writers we enjoy patterns made with words. The balancing of words and phrases in a paragraph, the sense of structure even when it's not visible, the seeking of aesthetic appeal in the look and sounds of words, poetic techniques such as rhyme and alliteration, the choice of first words and last words — all these are patterns of a verbal kind. Rather beautiful, too.

And so it goes.

65 THINGS TO DO

Think of an example of business writing that has really appealed to you. For example, I think of an advert I saw on the London tube to recruit people to join the VSO (Voluntary Service Overseas). It was an emotional piece of writing that achieved its effects through repetition, rhythm and rhyme. Analyze your chosen example, looking for the patterns that make the writing distinctive. Make a note of your observations, and think how you might use similar techniques in your next piece of writing.

Jamie to John

ON THE ROAD

I've travelled all my life, starting with dollar-a-day journeys through Africa, Asia Minor and South America in the late 1960s and early 1970s. I know very well how immersion in new landscapes and cultures alters one in subtle and sometimes unexpected ways. I also know how it provides an endless source of imaginative connections, as your example of Islamic art demonstrates.

But international business travel is something relatively new to me and it offers its own particular brand of metaphor. Last month I was in India, running communications training in Delhi and Hyderabad for a large Indian company. It was scorchingly hot — 48 degrees in Delhi when we arrived. Not that it made much difference to us, for this was travel of the most disconnecting kind — airport to hotel to training centre to hotel and so on, all in chauffeur-driven cars with the mean inside temperature of Scotland in March.

Beyond the windows the heat pounded down on cows, road-workers, beggars, motorcyclists, rickshaw drivers and pedestrians. We slid past them with a sense of suspended reality, aware that a fundamental part of India's soul was missing from our experience.

There was something essential missing from the way my client organisation spoke, too. Theirs is not the natural language of human exchange. Process, analysis, statistics and data are their currency; and the lack of human content is exacerbated by PowerPoint, which has become so widely used in the organisation that it has almost replaced conversation. The usual request is not so much 'come and talk to me' as 'send me some slides'.

In the training, I took people through a series of exercises designed to show them that anything, however small, that lit a spark in their audience's imagination would increase tenfold the human contact they made. There was a point at which understanding dawned, almost invariably followed by a smile and a look of longing; then a worried frown and a flood of questions, as reality impinged once more and they retreated to their positions as if inside the air-conditioned car, looking out at the hot, crowded, pulsating human world beyond, and wondering if they dared open the windows.

I reassured them that it would take courage to do it the first time, but that once they had, once they'd felt what happened when they let the metaphorical heat and smell and sounds rush in and wrap around them, there would be no going back.

What's your own personal metaphor for communicating well? If you don't have one, think back through your experiences of travel or sport or the arts — or even your education — and find something that expresses what you feel when you know you're really getting a message across. Then place your *bon mot* somewhere that you'll see it whenever you sit down to write.

Week 30
John to Jamie

THE REAL THING

Your description reminds me why I love theatre — surely the polar opposite of life seen through the windows of an air-conditioned car. Theatre is *live*, that's what defines it and that's its excitement. And what an important word *live* is.

I've been lucky enough to work with two great London theatre companies in helping express their brands: the National and the Old Vic. Most people's first thoughts are about theatrical flamboyance, but what I've learnt particularly from theatre is the obsession with detail and the way the theatre uses detail to make performance *live*. Actors, directors and playwrights rehearse, revise and rework constantly, each time trying to get that closer connection you refer to, the spark in the audience's imagination.

The Old Vic's played a big part in my life. I used to visit it regularly as a teenager to see the National Theatre that had its first theatrical home there. I remember vividly seeing Robert Stephens and Maggie Smith perform in *The Recruiting Officer*. In recent years, under Kevin Spacey's direction, I've worked with the Old Vic to help them and others see the theatre in a different light. Last month I went to the Old Vic to see the new production of Tom Stoppard's play *The Real Thing*, watching Toby Stephens, son of Robert and Maggie, plaing the main part.

Stoppard's play is, as always, clever, witty and thought-provoking. It's about honesty and deception in relationships, and also about the writer's role as a recorder and interpreter of reality.

The play makes you laugh and think. So does the programme, which had a spread on 'Writers on Writing', with different quotations such as:

> *Don't tell me the moon is shining; show me the glint of light on broken glass.*
>
> **Anton Chekhov**

You can relate this completely to writing for business. Don't shout at me about how fantastic and amazing your product is; show me how it makes a difference to my life through relevant details and specific stories.

> *I know nothing in the world that has as much power as a word. Sometimes I write one, and I look at it, until it begins to shine.*
>
> **Emily Dickinson**

We all often complain 'if only we had time'. And it's true, we don't. But we still owe it to ourselves, as well as to our clients, to try to find the word that will shine. It might be the word that defines a brand and opens up a whole world. To *live*.

63 THINGS TO DO

Take a play script. It can be the first one that comes to hand — Shakespeare, Beckett, Stoppard…. You'll see that it's written almost entirely in dialogue. Now add your own annotations, describing what an audience might be seeing with each line of the script. What are the movements, expressions and objects seen by the audience that could accompany the spoken words? Think how little we use dialogue in business writing. Should we use it more?

SHOW, DON'T TELL

Those shining words, those stories and relevant details, are vital parts of the process of showing which, rather than telling, is widely considered to be one of the first principles of good writing.

Of course, there are times when there's no substitute for telling, but the idea of showing, of allowing your reader to find things out for themselves, is a sound one, because what we discover or experience tends to engage our imaginations more sharply than anything we're told. Hence the glint of light on broken glass, rather than the moon described.

Recently I heard the novelist and historian, Antonia Fraser, on Radio 4's *Front Row*. She was speaking of her difficulty in reading aloud the love poem by her late husband, Harold Pinter, with which she concluded her memoir of their life together, *Must You Go?*

She had been persuaded, somewhat against her better judgement, to read the book for radio, she explained. In the end, it took her several attempts to master the neutral voice that concealed her personal feelings, and left listeners the room they needed to discover the emotion in the poem for themselves. 'The sob is in the story,' she said. 'It mustn't be in the voice.'

If the story's strong enough and the writing good enough, no one needs another voice metaphorically holding up cue cards with exclamation marks or sad faces. But as you say, John, it's a lesson many organisations still have to learn. The temptation to tell the world how innovative or robust or trustworthy or — most laughably — how passionate they are, continues to seem irresistible. Yet it sounds like a ham performance which at worst stretches credulity, at best provokes the response: 'I think I'll decide that for myself, thank you.'

Storytellers have known from time immemorial that an idea or message revealed has more power than one baldly stated. And for some organisations, business case studies can be a nod in that direction; though even then the fear that people will somehow miss the point can result in the 'lesson' being spelt out at the end in bold type.

But the truth is that we learn from stories as naturally as we breathe, whether they hold sobs or laughter, facts or ideas; and we learn best when the author isn't leaning over our shoulder pointing things out. The stories just need to be told with conviction — passion, if you prefer — or sometimes, conversely, with perfect calm, as Toni Morrison, the Nobel Prize-winning American novelist, says:

> *You can't use fiery language to describe a fire. You have to use quiet language so the fire can be seen.*

62 THINGS TO DO

Look at a typical business document — the CEO's statement in an annual report, say, or the home page of a corporate website — and analyse how much showing they're doing and how much telling. It will probably be 'tell'-heavy. Try rewriting it to include more 'show' — you might have to invent some of the detail.

Week 31
John to Jamie

THIS MIGHT HURT

The principles we've talked about apply especially to writing for brands. There's always a danger that the language of brand definition can become very bland and generic. 'Passionate' is a given because no one wants to suggest that they are lacking in passion for their job.

It's worth writers getting passionate about the words they use. For example, with Guinness we had 'communion' as one of the brand values. I still wonder how that got through, there are such (deliberate) religious connotations to the word, as well as the idea of people coming together to share, almost as a ritual. But at the same time we were talking about 'Believe' as the advertising sign-off, and about Guinness 'reflecting your inner strength'. It all sounds slightly dangerous, but it worked for the Guinness brand.

Those words set the scene and the themes for stories I then wrote about Guinness. One of them was the founding story of Arthur Guinness, a man who believed in what he was doing. I wrote about him standing on the barricades, pick axe in hand, defending his rights to use Dublin's water. Those details created a vivid picture and expressed something more memorable about the brand than a PowerPoint slide full of abstract terminology.

As a writer you have to be prepared to stand on the metaphorical barricades to defend particular words you choose for reasons other than mere 'telling'. In the last year I've been writing stories to help express the National Australia Bank's brand. We'd defined their purpose as 'fulfilling lives'. *So how do you do that? Give me some stories, true stories…*

One story emerged and I had to piece it together by talking on the phone to half a dozen people who'd been involved. In brief, the bank supported a community of aboriginal artists in the middle of Australia. They gave them funds, built a community centre, bought the paintings that the artists created. They then used some of the paintings on ATM machines. When I wrote the story I began with this first paragraph:

> *The sun hurts. You stand there in this desert landscape and the sun blazes so you feel it burning your skin, pressing down on you like hot metal. Even the aboriginal people avoid it. The Titjikala children stand in the shade of a goal post that casts the thinnest of shadows. Even in that shade it's 40 degrees.*

The first feedback I got was from one of the people who had been managing the project. 'It's a harsh opening. Can't we start by explaining what we did? And I really don't like the word "hurts" in an opening sentence.'

I asked if I'd written anything inaccurate or untrue? 'No, not really, but it's the tone.' I insisted the tone was right — you can only 'fulfil lives' if you understand the lives people lead. And, sometimes, life hurts; so you connect with people's real experiences of life rather than tell the corporate tale. The paragraph wasn't changed.

61 THINGS TO DO
How do you think the story of the Titjikala artists continued? Using the first paragraph above as a starting point, write a second paragraph.

Jamie to John

SHEEP AND GOATS

Simple telling, apart from on those occasions when there's no alternative, usually represents a failure of imagination. It might be fair to say that your rather unimaginative client felt uncomfortable because you were inviting readers to engage imaginatively with the tough lives of those aboriginal kids.

I recently flew to Geneva, where I was struck by two advertisements along the walkway from the aircraft to the terminal. The first was for a Swiss merchant bank. It had no imagery, just simple bands of burgundy, gold and black, along with a classic serif typeface, to intimate privilege and exclusivity. 'Imagine a bank that combines strength with dedicated service…' it exhorted us. That was all. It was banal, ineffably smug and — worst of all — rather than working to engage our imaginations it lazily and haughtily commanded us to switch them on ourselves.

Imagine one that doesn't, I thought, moved by irritation to apply the principle of opposites. It's an old but handy trick for separating the sheep from the goats. If the opposite of what is stated raises a hollow groan or a weary sigh, then the writer is probably, to continue in agricultural vein, trying to make a silk purse out of a sow's ear, or at the very least, a virtue out of the unremarkable. Strength and dedicated service, one would think, are the *sine qua non* of any Swiss bank. I walked on, thinking that the copywriter should have been made to eat *raclette* till his giblets congealed.

Straight ahead, at the end of the walkway, was another advertisement, a huge and arresting photograph of the Dents du Midi mountains raising their snowy slopes into a clear blue sky. 'Bienvenu à notre usine' ran the copyline. 'Welcome to our factory.' In the bottom corner was the Evian logo. That was all. But what a difference …

Perhaps most tellingly, it was the advertisement that showed not one shred of imagination that used the word 'imagine', whereas the Evian ad had plenty, and it trusted that we'd use ours to get their message, witty and thought-provoking as it was. The ability to appeal to the imagination is one of the essential qualities of all good writing, but it also takes imagination to achieve it; you can't simply order people to turn theirs on. But then one ad was for a Swiss bank, the other a French multinational…

60 THINGS TO DO

Swap the imagery of the two advertisements, giving Evian the bank livery and the bank the photo of the Dents du Midi. Then write new copy for each in a way that really engages the reader's imagination.

Week 32
John to Jamie

TONAL OPPOSITES

The principle of opposites is very useful, particularly when thinking about a brand's tone of voice. One of the first tone of voice programmes I initiated was for Marks & Spencer when they seemed to be in decline in the late 1990s. The main thrust of the programme was to get them to speak and write more conversationally. There was a formal bureaucratic tone in everything they did because they had got out of the habit of speaking in a natural one-to-one way with their customers. This was a store that, at that time, directed customers to 'Horticulture' on its signing system when people were looking for signs saying 'Flowers'.

So the tone of voice issues for this job were quite simple, many of them dealing with what to avoid. The words used in stores were generally sending signals that were the opposite of any retailer's intention. 'Till point', for example, sounds very functional and was easy to replace with the more direct 'Please pay here'. It was a particularly cold form of language. Part of this was, I believe, because M&S had grown so powerful in relation to its suppliers. Decades of having suppliers jump to M&S commands had institutionalised a shorthand form of language that had grown out of an unequal relationship between the buying department and suppliers. This became a problem, though, when the same language was transferred into the stores to be seen by increasingly resistant customers.

Anyway, M&S changed its language and its way of working in time. What we have now on high streets is often a generic retail-speak conveying 'friendly service'. It's useful to apply the opposite test to statements like, 'Our dedicated team of friendly advisers are more than happy to help'. Would any shop ever say the opposite? 'Our couldn't-care-less, aggressive staff are less than happy if you bother them.'

As we've said, the Innocent brand is much copied when it comes to tone of voice. They have a very distinctive style and a lot of brands now want to imitate them in inappropriate ways. 'Innocent are innocent and you're a multinational oil company.' We've both had conversations of that type with clients.

But tone of voice is a wide spectrum and often we have to write in a way that is close to the opposite of Innocent. I've just done some writing for an investment firm. They really don't want to say much at all — the character of the people and the brand they represent is taciturn. It's a multinational company too, so basic English is a leveller. Deriving the tone of voice from the brand definition (it's about discipline, analysis and a focus on performance), I've chosen to write in a way that is straightforward, clear and to the point. It's not easy (clarity never is) and it's not such fun to write but it is distinctive and true to their character.

59 THINGS TO DO

Which are the words you encounter most frequently in defining the tone of voice for a brand? Passionate? Personal? Friendly? Write a list of possible opposite values. Then use those words to think about other adjectives that are the opposite of them. Perhaps you will discover different words that can help you create a more distinctive tone of voice.

Jamie to John

IN CHARACTER

Talking of character, why, when businesses cannot possibly be anything more than the sum of the people who make them work, are most of them so reluctant to reveal anything about their 'most precious resource'?

Perhaps we get news that so-and-so will bring invaluable experience of such-and-such to Company X. Perhaps we read a stultifyingly bland profile of the marketing director, or an anodyne, platitudinous personal message from the chief executive. But who really are these people? What gets them out of bed in the morning? What kind of music do they listen to? What makes them inspire the people who follow them?

The reason most organisations' stories are so shockingly dull is that there's nothing in them to engage the emotions or imagination; yet business is about nothing if not human endeavour, which means perseverance and struggle, success and failure, falling out and making up — all the stuff of good fiction, you could say.

Not every business has an Arthur Guinness, admittedly, but most people lead interesting lives once one gets beyond the superficial, and to know a little more about them is to know a little more about the organisation.

Periodically I visit an acupuncturist called Wenbo Xu. He's a charming man who finds it hard to get his tongue round the English language, but he has a gentle manner, a lovely smile and he fixes me every time. Until recently I knew relatively little about him other than that he's in his 40s and married with two children. Then I asked him how he came to be a doctor, and this is what he told me.

When he was a teenager, two of his grandparents died — needlessly, but where he lived there wasn't the medical help to save them. He was very affected by this, and when the time came, he chose to study medicine so he could do his bit to make sure his other two grandparents lived long lives. But arriving at university he discovered they were teaching Chinese medicine, which seemed contrary to all the science he'd studied at school, and he hated it.

He returned home and told his parents. His father was horrified. 'You can't quit,' he said. 'You're the first member of our family to go to university. Not just that, you're the first person in the neighbourhood to go. Everyone here is so proud of you. Think of the shame.'

So he dutifully returned and five years later graduated in both Chinese and Western medicine. As the top student in his year, the head of acupuncture in the university hospital was keen to give him a job. But it was 1990 and the previous year he'd organised local support for the Tiananmen Square protesters. The head of his university department was a Communist Party man who duly blocked the appointment, and he was sent to a big hospital in another region. He did well there, setting up and running a whole new department, but he didn't like the politics and when the chance eventually arrived to come to the UK, he jumped at it.

At this point, he stopped and gestured at the little treatment cubicle. 'I don't have a big job now,' he said, 'and I don't earn a lot of money.' Then he smiled. 'But I am free.'

Next time I go to him for treatment I will see this delightful man in a completely different light. He may have told me his personal story, but he also runs a business and I'm his customer. Need I say more?

58 THINGS TO DO

Imagine you're head of communications for a large organisation. Think about how you might use 'character' to bring the brand alive to the world, by telling the stories of the people who work alongside you. Then swap hats. Now you're head of internal communications. How can you use similar stories to make your colleagues feel more engaged with the business?

Week 33
John to Jamie

IT MAKES A CHANGE

I'm now thinking about medicine as a result of your Chinese doctor. It's also that time of year, August, when we seek a bit of refreshment from the sometimes relentless pressure of working life. Writers need refreshment just like anyone else, otherwise you get in a rut and your writing becomes stale and formulaic.

For me it's not so much a case of having a complete rest (I get bored) as finding ways to change routines and change ways of thinking. In the old phrase, 'A change is as good as a rest'. A change helps you to make discoveries (particularly about yourself) and those discoveries refresh your approach to writing. I think it's the most exciting thing about getting older; you know that there's still so much more to discover if you keep pushing yourself to do so. Age is something you gain simply by being alive; experience you gain by living. But even as you get older you need to keep seeking new experiences.

So here's a change for our readers — 10 *things to do* instead of one. An entire summer break of things to do. Ten ideas that will help you make new discoveries as a writer and keep your writing fresh.

57 THINGS TO DO

Write in a style and genre you've never previously tried. If you've never written a sonnet, for example, try it. Or write a children's story. If you hate what you write there's no need to show it to anyone, it's just for you. But it will have influenced the way you write.

56 THINGS TO DO

Go to a part of the world you've never visited before to experience a completely different culture. The artists The Boyle Family threw darts into a big map of the world in the 1960s, and they've been making art works in the places where the darts landed ever since. Try a similar technique to decide where you might go.

55 THINGS TO DO

Go for a walk through a place you've never visited near where you live. Take a camera and use it to record details of your journey. The smallest details might be the most interesting. Assemble the pictures into a photo story. Don't feel that you need to add any words.

54 THINGS TO DO

Go to experience an art form you always told yourself you hated. Try to go with someone who loves that art form. The opera or ballet or performance poetry? You might be surprised — keep an open mind.

53 THINGS TO DO

Take a solo day-long train journey to and from a city
you've not visited before — take only a notebook
and write as you go about what you think and
observe along the way. It becomes more than a
physical journey.

52 THINGS TO DO

Have a meal in a restaurant whose style of cooking
you've not tasted before. How would you describe
the food you've just eaten? Write your response to the
meal in the style of that cuisine.

51 THINGS TO DO

Find out about an area of science that baffles you —
really try hard to work it out. When you've found out
(with at least a little greater understanding), explain it to
a child.

50 THINGS TO DO

Start learning a foreign language that you don't know.
It will change the way you think and write in English.

49 THINGS TO DO

Who lives in the neighbouring street at No. 26?
Imagine. Write about them.

48 THINGS TO DO

Visit an art gallery and choose a painting you admire.
Stand in front of it, study it, meditate on it, absorb its
effects. Then write the words you think the artist would
have written if he or she had chosen to 'write' the
painting instead of painting it.

Jamie to John

SPIRIT OF PLACE

Among other things, summer holidays bring the stimulation of new landscapes. If you've ever written a holiday or travel journal, it's more than likely that you made some attempt to capture the spirit of the place you visited. Your story would be incomplete without it.

But it's not only travel writing that deals with place. Looking across from my desk at the wall opposite, on one shelf containing 27 books — a random mixture of fact and fiction (because I haven't got round to sorting them out) — I can count 19 in which location plays a major part. In some writing, landscape or place is so prominent that it becomes a character in its own right. Dickens' London is just one obvious example.

But is there a place for 'place' in business writing? I'm convinced there is. Just as people's stories (like my acupuncturist friend's) help bring business messages to life, so too does a sense of location. It's one more thing that allows readers to connect imaginatively with the brand or organisation.

One of the good things about living in Scotland is that most of us who write end up working with the whisky industry sooner or later. Not only are many distilleries to be found in outstandingly beautiful locations, but their raw materials come directly from the land around them — the barley, the peat and the pure hill water. A sense of place is central to their stories, and it makes writing for them a pleasure. This is also true of many other types of business — tourism, food and other drinks, handcrafted and 'heritage' products, outdoor wear, green goods and so on.

But what about the service industries: banks or insurance companies, for example? Does occupation of a steel-and-glass tower in London's Docklands confer a particular character on a financial services company? Yes, of course it does. People who work in, say, Canary Wharf surely feel differently to people who work in, say, an historical district like Threadneedle Street. The place where they spend more than half their waking lives cannot fail to become part of how they define themselves, and the same must be true of the organisations they work for. So with a little imagination, the location can be given a role in the story.

I checked the website of the Dunfermline Building Society ('Scotland's Building Society' as it styles itself with the strapline: 'For a longer happier relationship'), to see whether it made anything of its less-than-immediately-obvious location in a very ancient town on the north side of the Firth of Forth — a town which nevertheless happens to be a former Scottish capital, has an abbey and was once the burial place of kings. But the only clue to the organisation's identity on the whole site (and believe me, I searched) was a description of it as 'a trading division of Nationwide Building Society' — which may explain everything.

But if I had my mortgage with them, I wouldn't mind knowing, for example, that Dunfermline was also the birthplace of the world's once-richest man, Andrew Carnegie, or that it was sacked in 1303 by English King Edward I, or simply what was going on in Dunfermline in 1869 that made the launch of a building society seem like a good idea. As you've said elsewhere, John, it's all about being able to find connections.

47 THINGS TO DO

Take a few minutes to do a little research on Canary Wharf. What was there originally? What was the developers' vision for regeneration? What is its physical relationship with the rest of the City? Then think how you might work this into the story of an imaginary bank that relocated there.

SPEAKING IN TONGUES

Every time I go away, I'm struck by the way the identity of the place is shaped by language. There are different versions of the English language — I'm sure Dunfermline has its own idiosyncratic version. One of the great joys of English is that it's a language of great variety, constantly changing and infinitely flexible. It's a beautiful chameleon of a language, and we should treasure it in all its forms.

We should treasure other languages, too. Travel makes you aware of the shifting plates of language. Language, whichever the particular form of a language in a specific place, evolves and also reflects our changing ways of thinking and being. Like Darwinian evolution, it seems to me something to admire and celebrate.

I went to Granada in southern Spain. What distinguishes this part of Spain is the still visible and audible influence of the Islamic culture that dominated this corner of Europe for eight centuries until the defeat of the Moors in 1492. (A significant year in history, with the Spanish *Reconquista* armies driving the Moors from the Iberian peninsula *and* Columbus' 'discovery' of the American continent.)

The Alhambra in Granada is a wonder of the world. It's an Islamic palace, fortress, town and gardens that still dominates the city panorama. I was interested in the way its name changed to reflect changing languages and cultures. Originally, it had a Celtic name that was eventually romanised to 'Illiberis'. When the migrating Visigoths arrived from the north they thought this equated to 'Elvira'.

Later it became known as 'Garnata el yehud', the 'hill of pilgrimage of the Jews', a reminder that there have been times when Islamic, Jewish and Christian communities could co-exist peacefully. The Arabs then called the place 'Kharnatta', but when the Christian kings expelled them this became 'Granada' in Spanish (because that's what it sounded like to them).

Granada happens to mean 'pomegranate' in Spanish. Early brand consultants then decided that the pomegranate would make an attractive visual symbol for the city. And five centuries later, you still see the pomegranate sign on public buildings.

Fruit always has metaphorical appeal. But in southern Spain fruits hang in the trees as you walk down the streets. I still find it wonderful to see oranges, lemons and even pomegranates growing among dark green leaves. You can almost hear *una naranja* passing from Spanish into French as *une orange* before forming between English lips as 'an orange'. So familiar now, even as a mobile phone company let alone a once exotic fruit, orange still reminds us subtly of its foreign origins in our language. It does so through its reluctance to rhyme with any other English words.

Can you think of an English word to rhyme with orange?

46 THINGS TO DO

Take a recent paragraph of your own writing. Think about every word you have used in that paragraph and question the origins of each word, using a good dictionary. When it comes to words, English has had a very open immigration policy, and that receptiveness has enriched the language. How many of the words in that paragraph are 'foreign' in origin?

Jamie to John

FINDING YOUR VOICE

If language is one of the most distinctive features of national identity (just imagine France without French, or Italy without Italian), the way we speak as individuals is certainly one of the most distinctive features of our personalities. In fact, I'd go further and say that our physical voices are perhaps the single most powerful mark of identity we have. We will recognise a voice long after we've forgotten the detail of its owner's appearance.

Our metaphorical voices are also a unique and powerful expression of who we are. As writers, we have to find our own before we can competently give voices to others; we have to know, and have confidence in, the way we communicate our authentic selves to the world beyond. You've mentioned how in workshops you invite people to write a short piece expressing a strongly held opinion. This is an excellent way of listening to our own writers' voices. So, too, are those short bursts of 'automatic' writing, when we write fast, without thinking, and set aside all the baggage we usually bring to the writing process.

Sometimes the opportunity for a more elaborate approach presents itself. A few years ago I took part in 'The Bard & Co', a 26 project which asked writers to explore modern business communications through the medium of a Shakespeare play. One of my clients at the time was Gillian Clelland, an enterprising and imaginative communicator, then with the drinks company, Scottish & Newcastle. I invited her and her internal communications team to join in with me.

My play was *Romeo & Juliet* — which, as it happens, is about nothing if not a failure of communication. I allocated each member of the eight-strong team a character in the play and sent them off to read it. When we met again, the first thing almost everyone admitted to was having struggled with the language. It's hard to think of anything that strikes a greater contrast with the flaccid language of modern business than Shakespearian English; and that in itself, though unintended, proved to be a valuable part of the exercise, forcing people not only to tune their ears to Shakespeare's linguistic richness and unravel his layered meanings, but to think much harder about the shortcomings of their own use of language.

The next step was a day trip to Stratford to see a Royal Shakespeare Company production of the play. Finally, I asked them each to write a piece explaining what their allocated character had to tell them about the modern business world. When we met for the last time to hear the resulting essays, short stories, dialogues and monologues, it turned out that there were parallels aplenty; no one had to look far to find Montagues and Capulets, Mercutios and Tybalts, Romeos and Juliets, Nurses and Friars in this large modern organisation.

For my little group of business communicators, this was a writing experience completely out of the ordinary. It gave them the scope to be creative and imaginative, to look at a familiar world through a wholly new lens and, perhaps most importantly, to be free to relinquish the corporate mindset and listen to their own voices as writers. Just recently I met up with one of them again, and she told me that she remembered the project as one of the highlights of her career. That's how important it is to hear your own voice from time to time.

45 THINGS TO DO

Think of an incident that has recently struck you at work, whether personal or corporate, trivial or monumental. Now write it as if it were fiction, in the first person, from the perspective of one of the people involved.

Week 35
John to Jamie

MUSIC TO YOUR EARS

I loved 'The Bard & Co', too. In the project's introduction my task was to draw some lessons from Shakespeare's work to apply to business writing — and to do that particularly through the *Sonnets*. The lessons are too many to recap here but I'll focus on the abiding one for me.

The language, to modern ears, is difficult. But it is also music. That for me was the main message: we need to listen more to the music in the words we read and write. It's a hard point to get across because the business imperative tends to be 'get it down, get it out'. As long as meaning is conveyed, that's all right, isn't it?

I'd say, not really. Meaning is subtly changed by the smallest shift of words in an English sentence. Here's a phrase I just read in a novel. It's a perfectly ordinary, simple phrase; it would be accepted readily by plain English campaigners.

...they knew all about him.

But my eye had jumped in the reading (something that can happen even more when you read on screen than on the page) and I'd taken it as:

...they all knew about him.

The placing of the tiny word 'all' is crucial to our understanding of the meaning. That meaning could shift again if we rearranged the words one more time:

...all they knew about him.

My point is that the writer's first duty is to convey meaning, and we need to appreciate (and exploit) how subtle changes of words can radically alter meaning. But there is also the sound. When you move the word 'all', you also change the metre and you hear a different rhythm in the words. So you have to consider, once satisfied with meaning, whether the sound supports or hinders that meaning.

I'm currently working with a digital design agency called 3Sixty, based in Bristol. They're very good at what they do but have struggled to articulate what that is. The term 'digital' is important to them but it's limiting; they're keen to convey that it's thinking rather than technology that sets them apart. In brief, they create websites that work hard. They start from the way users gain value from the site, then design it to make it as easy and useful as possible. Now we've agreed that the concept of 'useful beauty' represents the essence of what they do: this is their brand.

They wanted a strapline — or at least something descriptive that would appear on their own website. I was thinking about this as the train carried me along the tracks between Bristol and London. The railway rhythm was in my head. The words came out as: *useful, usable, beautiful, digital.* The meaning was right but it was the rhythm that made it right.

44 THINGS TO DO

In the film *The King's Speech* the speech therapist (played by actor Geoffrey Rush) at times gets King George (Colin Firth) to sing parts of the speech in rehearsal. It's a way of getting over the king's terrible stammer. Try singing some of your own writing (lock yourself away somewhere private!). Does it have a natural music?

Jamie to John

FAKING IT

Rhythm in writing is one of the 'enhancing' qualities. You can understand the sense of what is being said without it, though its absence, like the absence of pace or colour, leaves the writing feeling flat and functional. At best, as in your railway example, it can be what brings everything else together into something greater than the sum of the parts. But in music, if you take away the rhythm you're usually left with something that makes no sense at all. Try and imagine Rossini's *William Tell Overture* without those galloping hooves, the Gershwin brothers' *I Got Rhythm* without the swing, or Michael Jackson's *Thriller* without that driving, menacing pulse.

I've played music semi-professionally all my life, first as a guitarist, latterly as a pianist. I'm a naturally rhythmic player, and that part of the musical structure comes easily to me. I'm also lucky to have a good ear — I can listen to things and reproduce them quickly — so I have an intuitive understanding of musical theory derived from many years of hearing what works and what doesn't. But as a result I've never really learnt to read music. Working out a melody from the dots is laborious, while reading a two-handed part is quite beyond me.

A few years ago I decided it was time I learnt to play the jazz standards. Much of what goes on in them is too complicated to be able to register accurately by ear alone (for me, at any rate), so I resorted to every jazz player's fall-back, the fake books. These wonderful volumes set out the song on a single page, two at most, so there's never any need for page-turning. They have the melody notated, usually in the treble clef only; the normal directions, such as repeats, bridges and codas; and, crucially for jazz players, the chord symbols above each bar — for example, $Am^{7(b5)}$ which means the chord of A minor seventh with a flattened fifth.

A typical righthand jazz chord is composed of four notes, but it can be played in any number of inversions — in other words, you might choose to put the A of $Am^{7(b5)}$ at the bottom, or somewhere in the middle, or at the top of the chord. Full musical notation would specify which inversion you played. But the fake books leave you to play the chord any way you like, and also to improvise around it, while preserving the basic tonal and harmonic texture of the song.

It strikes me that the fake books offer something not dissimilar to a tone of voice guide. They ensure that the integrity of melody and structure are not compromised while allowing you plenty of scope to bring your own interpretation to the accompaniment — in the same way that a business's tone of voice sets out to embody their essential organisational values, while leaving its spokespeople free to bring their individual personalities to bear in the way they express its messages. The result, in the best of both cases, is something that feels spontaneous and heartfelt rather than laboured and contrived. But you do have to know your way around the keyboard, or vocabulary, for either to work.

43 THINGS TO DO

Find a glossary of jazz terms (there are plenty online) and see where you can find parallels in writing. For example, what would be the literary equivalent of syncopation?

Week 36

John to Jamie

REVOLUTION OR EVOLUTION?

Jazz was revolutionary music in its time. We form our musical tastes — generally in our adolescent years — and we tend to stick with them for life. But, with words, with music, it's always good to challenge yourself to try new forms, as you've been doing.

David Byrne (the singer/songwriter in the band Talking Heads) is a constant seeker of new musical and artistic possibilities. Last summer I went to his show 'Playing the building' at the Roundhouse. David Byrne was there, now grey-haired, looking a little bashful as he wandered around while the audience (guests at this strange party) took turns at the old pump organ that had been installed at the centre of the floor under the vast dome. We were invited to *play the building*.

Which meant what? The organ was the focal point of a sound installation — an installation that involved the whole of the cavernous Roundhouse building (in Victorian times it used to be a train shed). The Roundhouse became a giant musical instrument played by people pressing the keyboard or pulling the stops on the organ. The 'music' was not conventional. The organ played no notes — instead it activated movement through the leads that were attached to it. These movements set off devices linked to the physical frame of the building — its pipes, beams, conduits. Through wind, vibration or striking, they produced noise. And the noise swirled, clanked, dinged, banged, sighed around you. The building came alive.

It really wasn't music. But it was a strangely moving experience. I thought of it as trying to create the internet by using only 19th century mechanical means.

I'm sure that a century on from now, human beings will look back at the internet as we know it and they will smile patronisingly. But here and now we have new developments daily that potentially change our lives. For the business writer, apart from the internet itself (strange how it's so quickly become such a part of the way we live), there are also social media. Facebook and Twitter are prime examples. Perhaps they are similar to jazz, with their ability to give us freer, looser forms of expression.

Social media are changing communication. They allow everyone to have a voice, and that voice can be a more public one than previous generations would have found comfortable. King George VI might well have stammered when confronted by Twitter's facility in revealing the ordinariness inside us all. I'm not sure where Twitter will lead but I think it's important, as writers, that we join in and explore its potential. That potential might prove to be more personal than corporate.

For me, almost inevitably, it's the constraint in using 140 characters that attracts. Not a set number of words but an absolute limit on characters (including character spaces). This will lead to something, perhaps a completely new form of writing, but for now we are just experimenting, waiting for the jazz symphony to emerge in words.

42 THINGS TO DO

Write a story using the Twitter constraint. Just 140 characters — no more. We set this challenge to a Dark Angels group last year and below we show their responses. Write a story about a 'lost moment' in 140 characters.

Gardens of Granada. Pomegranate gleams in green leaves, BlackBerry dims. No more e-mails. No more Moors. A last sigh. E-mails back to sender. John

Pin-striped legs, marching in time. Eyes forward, arms loaded. A red coat breaks up the City grey. She catches me watching. I look away. Anelia

Soldier shirt. leotard. fishnet stockings. cap over glint in your eye. stage call. slinking shrug. eyelash flashing. twinkling wink goodbye. Andy

O guru! O method! O teacher! O pregnant promise of learning! Burning figments of the mutual. 'Read this' she said, 'and let it spur you on.' Chris

I thought that you had kept me waiting, until I realised that you had, through waiting, kept me. Martin

Cool clear cloudless. Soft sun. Tokyo London. Autumn's Platonic conception of itself. Wouldn't it be great if it was like this all the time? Neil

Quite a character/Though notable by absence/Giving pause for breath/He's the unseen guest/But it's not hard to find him/He'll be at the bar. Paul

Thoughts spin like crazy plates. Shadows at a circus. I wait, breathing…willing the din to die away. Waiting for you to come, and slow. Me. Down. Where are you, Mr Sleep? Heather

MMMaaa. Shlooo. Door. Door! Key! Key! Keeeeeeeey! Hoooovah. Bagga. Bagga. Bagga! Hahum. Hah. Car! Wayawaya. Bye-bye, bye-bye. MMMaaaaaaaa. Claire

Taxi out: wait: taxi back: taxi out: wait: back: disembark: wait in bus: several bottle out: climb stairs: taxi out: take off: for starters. Stuart

The King & I. And me in the wings. I'm guard/peasant/priest; cloud, half a house and a guy called Phra Alack. Harborough Theatre needs men. Thomas

Indian dawn. Half asleep. Luggage on platform. Train leaving station. Where's the camera? Oh no...oh well...one happy sleeping car attendant. Jamie

Jamie to John

YOU HAVE MAIL ...

At some point during most workshops I run, someone pipes up with: 'What about e-mail?'. 'What about it?' I reply. 'Well, what's the right way to use it?' A little probing usually reveals two things: one, that its informality makes a lot of people feel nervous; and two, that almost everyone has some story of a hastily sent e-mail causing offence.

Hard though it is to imagine now, my working life began firmly in the era of snail mail. If you needed to contact someone you either telephoned them or wrote them a letter. If it was really urgent you used a courier (fax machines came later). There was still a certain gravitas about a letter; it had a degree of formality. Correct styles of address and salutation mattered. The thing had a physical form, ink had been applied to it, you had to remove it from its envelope and hold it in your hand as you read it before, most likely, filing it away in a folder in a metal cabinet — a process that when I started my first job, in the early 1970s, had probably not changed for over a hundred years.

Then came e-mail, and suddenly you could conduct an exchange with someone that had almost all the immediacy of an actual conversation, but with the one critical difference that you weren't face to face. So, unable to gauge the other person's response, reliant only on potentially slippery and ambiguous words, people found themselves unsure of how to behave. Forests have since been felled and fortunes doubtless made publishing guidance on the conventions and etiquette of e-mailing.

In the workshops, once we've established the particular uncertainties and anxieties, my response tends to be along these lines: e-mail makes us all enormously more connected and allows us to communicate instantaneously, wherever we are; but for those very reasons it places more pressure on our personal resources, and used mindlessly — for example, always copying everything to everyone — it can become an unwarranted intrusion. Like many great inventions, it's a mixed blessing whose benefits are directly proportionate to the intelligence and consideration with which it's used (which was probably also said of the first postal service).

So the answer to the question, 'How should we use it?' is really: 'How do you think you should? It's up to you.' Ultimately e-mail is no more than another medium of communication, and all the basic human considerations and courtesies still apply. Use your judgment as you would with any other kind of writing in business. Know your reader or readers. Send the e-mail you would like to receive. And pause for reflection before hitting 'send'.

41 THINGS TO DO

Take a recent e-mail you've written and write it by hand on a sheet of paper, setting it out exactly as if it were a letter you were going to mail. Notice what differences there are, what changes you would make and why.

DOWN TO THE FEW

Letters still matter to me. I used to write the Letterbox gift for the Royal Mail, a beautifully designed piece of print, different every year, given to all the children (nearly half a million of them) who took part in an annual letter-writing competition. Now the letter writers have dwindled to a few. All the more reason for thinking of the tactical use of a letter. I now send them occasionally when I really want someone to notice what I'm saying. It works. It's real Room 121 writing — one human being to another.

Of course, letters are not necessarily one-to-one, there are mass mailings and standard responses. The story in Jonathan Powell's book (*The New Machiavelli*) about Tony Blair amused me. Blair's father, Leo, sent his son a letter to Downing Street in the early days of his premiership, signed 'Your loving pa'. By mistake it went off, along with thousands of others, to the government department dealing with prime ministerial replies. The reply began: 'Dear Mr Loving Pa, Your views have been noted…'

In the last few days, to commemorate the 70th anniversary of the Battle of Britain, Radio 4 took the unusual step of playing five minutes, uninterrupted, of Churchill's speech that contained the words, 'Never in the field of human conflict was so much owed by so many to so few'. I stopped eating breakfast to listen, riveted by the compelling urgency of the tone. I imagined others doing the same in 1940. Except that it was afterwards explained that the only way to have heard the speech at the time was to be an MP in the House of Commons. What I'd listened to was the recording Churchill had made, for archive purposes, in a BBC studio in 1951.

There are many remarkable things about this. First, although Churchill's voice is so distinctive, speech writing was a literary activity for him. He wrote to be read. He read his speech as a letter to the nation. Next day you could read the speech in the national newspapers. The papers noted that the MPs cheered the famous soundbite about 'the few'. But the many didn't hear his words.

It shows how life has changed during a lifetime. The thought of such a speech — or major news of any kind — not being immediately available is now strange to contemplate. Why didn't they use the internet? (!)

Of course the internet has changed everything. It enables us to communicate instantly across time and distance. We have machines that are TVs, radios, shops, libraries, newspapers, post offices, telephones all rolled into one tiny device. It's a scientific miracle that has changed our lives. We couldn't live without it. But think occasionally about writing and sending a letter: it might work better for you simply because it's now a means of communication practised by the few, that can be targeted at the individual.

40 THINGS TO DO

When the inflation rate goes above target, the Governor of the Bank of England has to write a letter to the Chancellor of the Exchequer to explain why. Imagine that you are the Governor, and the news is very bad. How would your letter begin?

Jamie to John

UP CLOSE AND PERSONAL

There's an assumption in much of what we've discussed in this book that in business we're writing, as Churchill did, to be read. But what about writing designed to be heard? What about those millions, probably billions, of words that are spoken every day in presentations, at conferences, on video and broadcasts? Those words also require careful thought and crafting, and a real desire to connect in an immediate and human way. Yet when, in business, did you last hear someone speak who really lit a spark rather than sending you to sleep? And how did they do it?

The starting point, I'm convinced from my own experience both as a reader of historic speeches and as a writer or polisher of speeches for business leaders, is a sense of intimacy. No matter whether there's an audience of 10 or 10,000 people, the best speeches are written as if the speaker is face to face with just one of them.

Here's an example from Apple and Pixar founder Steve Jobs, speaking at Stanford University's graduation ceremony in 2005. The speech has become a classic. He begins it like this:

Today I want to tell you three stories from my life. That's it. No big deal. Just three stories.

He goes on to describe how he went from adoption to dropout to entrepreneur to cancer survivor. He speaks directly from the heart and reveals his vulnerability as a living, breathing, bleeding human being. There's no business-speak, no education-speak. His language is simple and conversational. His personal authenticity is beyond question and his intent is unambiguous and apparently without an agenda: he wants people to be inspired by his story to believe in themselves.

We've talked a lot about the importance of personality in writing and Steve Jobs' speech takes the notion about as far as you can go. But that sense of intimacy can still be present when the subject is much broader and potentially a lot drier. In autumn 2009, President Obama went before American Congress to argue for his hugely divisive health care bill; it was a monumental moment and a very serious topic. This is how he began:

When I spoke here last winter, this nation was facing the worst economic crisis since the Great Depression. We were losing an average of 700,000 jobs per month. Credit was frozen. And our financial system was on the verge of collapse.

As any American who is still looking for work or a way to pay their bills will tell you, we are by no means out of the woods.

Again, the language is simple, direct, conversational, yet there's no absence of gravitas, no loss of sense of occasion. Those five short, powerful sentences are replete with images of bleakness — *winter, crisis, depression, frozen, collapse, the woods* — which he dispels with a growing sense of optimism as the speech progresses. There isn't the slightest trace of government-speak. You are hearing the man, Barack Obama, and his personal conviction, and he could be talking in a bar in a small Midwestern town, rather than in the national debating chamber. He won the debate.

The art of speech writing is a book in itself, but the basic principles are just the same as those of writing to be read, though more so. Impact is crucial because once uttered the words are gone: you only get one shot at a speech. But authenticity and conviction are equally essential — and those will never be present if you, or the speaker you're writing for, are afraid to reveal your personalities, afraid of getting up close and personal with your audience.

39 THINGS TO DO

We've previously mentioned TED (Technology, Entertainment and Design) as a website that shows clips of inspiring speakers in practically any field of human endeavour you can think of. Take a couple of hours off to visit TED (at www.ted.com) and be inspired — but also think hard about what these speakers are doing. Make notes. Learn from them.

SPEAKING AS A WRITER

I always follow US Presidential elections because I'm fascinated by the language and speeches. If I say I'm drawn towards Presidents Kennedy, Clinton and Obama, it's partly political preference but more particularly me placing my vote for the writers. It's also why I love the TV show *The West Wing*, so much of it is actually about writing.

Writers might have to write speeches for themselves or for others to deliver. Writing for someone else is always trickier. You're putting words in someone else's mouth. It's important to know the person a little and to try to have a conversation (even though you've probably been asked to write the speech because the speaker 'just doesn't have the time'). In your short time with the speaker, elicit stories; try to include at least one or two real ones in the speech.

Soon after Kevin Spacey became artistic director at the Old Vic, I was asked to write a speech for him to be delivered at a dinner about 'marketing the arts'. The previous week there had been tabloid news and diary pieces appearing because Kevin had lost his phone while walking at night. The tabloids were smelling a scandal, but fortunately it was blowing over by the time of the speech. It gave me a good way to start, referring to the story. Knowing the audience would be on his side, it was safe to get under way with a self-deprecating laugh that could lead on to a serious point.

I was talking on my mobile phone the other day — fortunately I now have a replacement — and the thought occurred to me: how fast communications have changed. Ten years ago mobile phones, text messages, e-mails were still novelties.

But then the second thought occurred to me: actually very little has changed except technology. Communication, marketing, still depends on two people making human connection with each other — to find out something that they'll both find interesting.

Of course, we're not all Kevin Spacey. But we do need to act a little when delivering a speech, and many of us find that an uncomfortable experience. I used to hate it but now, whether through increased confidence or egotism, I've grown to enjoy delivering public speeches. I enjoy the performance, and we need to remember that all writing is a kind of performance.

Most people in companies who ask me to help with speeches have PowerPoint presentations in mind. We've all been on the receiving end of bad presentations. Why are they bad? Generally, they lack human personality — no stories. The fault is not with PowerPoint but with the way it is used. There is no point in putting up slide after slide, with six bullet points per slide, and then reading out to your audience what they can read for themselves on the screen. With PowerPoint, images are effective (choose photos that make your point and speak to them) and single words or very short phrases (use big, bold typography).

You might have a script — if you're a writer you probably will have a script — and you might lack the confidence not to read directly from it. It's unlikely that you'll have an autocue. There is no point trying to memorise then recite every word: your delivery will be wooden as you worry about forgetting a word or phrase. So relax, let yourself read the script. The images on the screen will be a positive distraction for your audience but you must look up regularly from your script. Eye contact is vital. The audience members of any of those American presidents will tell you that the president's eyes were frequently on them.

38 THINGS TO DO

Find a recent US president's speech and notice the rhetorical techniques used. To help you spot them, speak the speech in front of a mirror. While looking, exaggerate the actions, expressions and gestures that might accompany the words. Then close your eyes and say the lines you remember inside your head. Listen to them, then think why you remember them.

HUMAN CAPITAL

You mention *The West Wing*. At the risk of starting to sound like two peas in a pod, I must also own up to being an addict, if a latecomer, to this brilliant TV series. My wife and I are currently about halfway through and watching it every spare evening we have. As you say, a great deal of the pleasure is to be had from the writing, which is intelligent, witty, thought-provoking and sometimes very powerful emotionally.

I remember an early episode in which the deputy chief of staff meets with a black senator who wants the government to start making reparations for slavery. As their exchange grows increasingly heated, the senator describes how his own ancestors were kidnapped in West Africa, transported across the Atlantic in appalling conditions and sold onto a plantation. Clearly discomforted, the deputy chief of staff suggests that the conversation would be better kept in the abstract. But the senator demurs, knowing his emotional case is a powerful one.

Most business leaders, like public servants, are fearful of emotion. They like abstractions because they take the heat out of uncomfortable realities. 'Shrinking markets', for example, seems somehow more palatable than 'fewer customers'. We've touched on this theme of abstraction versus concrete reality before, I know, but in the context of speeches and presentations it becomes even more pressing. For when we see and hear people using language like this at the podium or in front of a PowerPoint screen, the sense of disconnection is amplified. The part of my brain that simply goes to sleep when all I'm being asked to do is read the stuff, now sits bolt upright and says: human beings should *not* be speaking like this.

I recently heard for the first time of what strikes me as a particularly revolting abstraction. In certain circles – most likely among those large, dysfunctional organisations, often the product of mergers, whose leaders have lost all sense of real connection with their employees — 'human capital' is the latest tag for the people without whose talents and energy there would be no business in the first place. But then you can 'reduce your capital' with an easier conscience than you can lay people off.

Slaves, of course, were human capital in the most literal sense. If I knew who they were, I would ask the people who coined the term (and the irony is that they're most likely to be in human resources) to reflect on that for a moment, because as Orwell so brilliantly demonstrated, you can enslave people with language, and particularly the language of abstraction, just as easily as you can with chains.

37 THINGS TO DO

There's a certain inevitability about this one: watch *The West Wing*. If you already have, invest in one of the other big US TV drama series — *Six Feet Under, The Sopranos, The Wire, Mad Men* — and really pay attention to the writing: it's in a class of its own. Keep a notebook handy. Over several months' viewing, some of it should start to rub off!

Week 39

John to Jamie

DARK ANGELS FLY

Let's move from being enslaved by language to being liberated by it. We are just about to fly, literally and metaphorically. Why? Because we are heading for our annual Dark Angels week in Andalucia, where we gather a group of 10 business writers from different backgrounds and places. This year we have participants flying in from the US, Australia, Denmark and Sweden, as well as from the UK. For everyone it's a chance to spread their wings in their writing: to take risks in a supportive atmosphere; to explore new possibilities; to cast off the shackles of a business world that often confines people to a narrow, unimaginative style of communication.

So why did we call ourselves *Dark Angels?* The long answer is in the book I wrote with that title, but you recently put it well in a few words.

It's a nod to Milton's Paradise Lost *and the idea that our creativity comes from our flawed human nature; that as Dark Angels we are neither those who have ascended nor those who have fallen, but that we occupy the fertile, if broken, territory somewhere in between.*

It's about each of us as writers expressing our humanity and making links with the humanity in others. Corporate communication can act as a deterrent to such thinking, because it seems less 'safe'. People used to say, no one got sacked for buying an IBM computer. It was the safe choice, even though other choices might offer you more possibilities. Try buying an IBM computer now. So there is an element of subversiveness in what we do.

But if we encourage small uprisings in the business world we justify it on two grounds. First, it is good for the individuals concerned — they emerge from a Dark Angels course transformed, with greater confidence and enjoyment of their own writing ability. They emerge proudly as writers.

The second justification is that the approach works in business terms. No business benefits from ineffective communication, which we might call bad writing. If businesses are producing words that make little human connection, they are failing to make the most of their potential. As you were saying about 'human capital', Jamie: there's really no point in businesses proclaiming 'people are our greatest assets' if they then deny them opportunities to show what really makes them an asset — that is, to express their individual personalities through the words that they use.

So I'm looking forward to arriving at Finca El Tornero de Abajo and starting to work with this group of writers. This year we have global brand directors, senior marketing executives, business owners, communication consultants and freelance writers. It's a mix we've encountered before, and we know it works. In our first session we'll come together on the terrace and explore stories of arrival, starting with an exercise based on a classic Spanish story. But we'll get people underway with a quick-fire exercise that makes the fundamental point: facts inform; arguments persuade; stories involve. So let's tell a story.

36 THINGS TO DO

After your next journey — on foot, by bus or boat or bike, by train or plane, however you travel — take 10 minutes to do the following, very quickly. First, write down the factual details of your journey, being specific. Then write why you chose to travel using that particular mode or route. Then write about something or someone that caught your attention during the journey. Which of these three observations would you pass on — and to whom?

Jamie to John

TUNING UP

There are several collective nouns for angels: a host, an exultation, a chorus, a choir. So among other things, angels can be numbered by reference to sound. Although we hadn't made the connection when we decided on the name, it's one of those wonderfully serendipitous titles that helps bring meaning to the apparent randomness of the world around us. For Dark Angels is about nothing if not helping people to find their voices.

The *finca* is the Spanish home of my childhood friend, novelist Robin Pilcher. A chestnut farm on a hillside in the Sierra de Aracena, it's a place of magical light, long views to distant ridges, tumbling wooded slopes and clear, clean air. We wake there to a morning chorus of dogs, roosters and a donkey, their calls echoing up from the valley as it floods with sunlight. And there's another sound when the Dark Angels are gathered there: the sound of human voices raised together in celebration of existence.

We work on the principle that our physical and metaphorical voices (as writers) are two halves of a whole, and that if you exercise one you're also exercising the other. So the day begins with five minutes of singing, usually a simple but beautiful early Christian chant: *Ubi caritas et amor, deus ibi est* (where there is kindness and love, there is god).

Religion has never had any place on our courses and never will, but that's not to say it can't offer us a rich seam of music and language. The almost nursery rhyme-like melody of *Ubi caritas* is easy to learn and the sentiment is one that most people find hard to disagree with, even though some might prefer to substitute the word 'truth' for 'god'. Most importantly, though, the chant brings us together in a way that these days is all too rare.

Once upon a time the human voice was the predominant sound wherever one walked on earth, but today it's drowned out by machines, and even when it's not, half of us go about with our ears blocked by headphones. But at Finca el Tornero, our voices ring out in unison across the valley, the chant at once a confluence of sounds, a raising of consciousness and an invocation. It brings us together in a way that reminds us of both our individuality and our shared humanity. It's good for our lungs and our heads, our hearts and our souls.

And when we come to the other exercises, that word 'kindness' is at the root of everything we teach, for kinder words are those that work harder to recognise our human kinship. As you've just said, John, nothing is more vital to good writing or any other kind of communication, and yet it's so often missing in the world from which our students come — the world of business. Each year we watch them drink at the well of kindness like desert travellers at an oasis; and as the sweet water soothes their parched throats we hear their voices growing stronger.

35 THINGS TO DO

If you sing, consider joining a choir. If that seems like a step too far, learn some songs that you can sing to yourself when you're driving or walking or alone in your home. And if you're definitely not a singer, learn some poems and get into the habit of declaiming them aloud whenever you can. It's not as strange as it might sound!

Part 4

AUTUMN

John to Jamie

THERE'S A PLACE

I've stayed on in Spain for a little break after our time with the Dark Angels. Last week was exhausting but uplifting. The memory is strong of people at Finca El Tornero reading their words as they strolled back and forth in a line across the courtyard, reproducing the atmosphere of the Aracena *paseo*. It showed that people had really absorbed the place itself and let it into their writing.

One of the group, Julian, is an expert in 'place marketing' and has helped rebrand many cities. It's an aspect of branding that has grown in the last two decades, perhaps fuelled by the commercial spur of the Olympic movement, but it's always been there throughout history. In fact, Olympia once did a fine job in marketing itself to the whole of Greece and beyond. A decade ago at Interbrand, I was part of the team that was asked to rebrand London. We wanted to use the campaign line 'We are London' but it was rejected. Now it's slightly galling to see an Adidas advertising campaign on the London Underground that uses just that line.

But here I am in Seville, a city that staged an Expo in the 1920s, largely as a means of marketing itself to the world. Cities and countries create brands and stage events to encourage business development and tourism, and for my time in Seville I'm relieved to be a tourist. New places provide food for the imagination and Seville's an appetising city. Perhaps it's the sunshine but I can feel myself being restored as I walk around: taking in the smell of oranges, Flamenco dancers clapping in rehearsal inside buildings, gold glittering in the cathedral, the cool touch of water in the fountains. Even better if I sit with a coffee, pencil in hand, notebook on table.

Where do you write? It seems that there are articles constantly in the newspapers about 'writers' rooms'. The message seems to be that there's a magic to the physical space where a writer writes. So, the implication goes, create such a space for yourself, probably at home (or a shed in your garden), make it idiosyncratic and personal. A photograph might accompany the article showing certain items: photographs pinned to the wall, posters, objects collected on travels, gifts from other writers.

All those things are important. I enjoy writing in my own study at home, surrounded by objects that matter to me. I sit at a desk without a computer (that's in another room) because I always produce first drafts by writing on paper with a pencil.

But the space itself is not everything. We shouldn't allow ourselves to think we can write only when surrounded by the personal talismans of our craft. If so, we might create the opposite result from the one we seek: we might just be beckoning writer's block to come and join us.

What matters is finding the right zone, but the zone is inside our heads. I've written before of techniques that I use to find that zone. These include a physical change of location, a burst of automatic writing, going for a run. When doing any of these activities, I often find myself in a different mental zone, where ideas and words are flowing much more easily. I might be in that zone but I'm not always aware of it. It's a wonderful feeling when you're there and then you realise afterwards that you've been there. I guess it's part of the addiction of being a writer.

34 THINGS TO DO

Go to a place where you've never been before. It could be a coffee shop, a train, at the top of a monument, beneath a tree in a wood. Just take a notebook and pencil. Record your thoughts about a project in the form of a to-do list. Write as freely as you can, without editing and see where your thoughts take you.

FREE TO CHOOSE

Earlier this year, when we were working on the '26:50' project and paying tribute to International PEN's imprisoned writers, I found myself constantly trying to imagine the circumstances in which they managed to write: where they found and concealed their materials, how they avoided the scrutiny of guards, from what miraculously still-luminous corners of their hearts they managed to summon the words.

In the free world, the choice of where and how, let alone what, we write is something we take for granted. Here's Hemingway:

> *It was a pleasant café, warm and clean and friendly, and I hung up my old waterproof on the coat rack to dry and put my worn and weathered felt hat on the rack above the bench and ordered a café au lait. The waiter brought it and I took out a notebook from the pocket of the coat and a pencil and started to write.*

Most unusually for rural Scotland, I live within walking distance of both a small community arts centre with an excellent café, and a mainline railway station. These days I write less and less in my converted garage at home — to echo your point, it has definitely, after seven years, gone stale on me — and more and more in either the café or on the train. In each case I draw energy from my surroundings.

On the train it's both the movement itself that encourages my words to flow, and the sense of moving through a world I can see but from which I am temporarily isolated. In the café it's the feeling of being fixed in a particular corner of the world but not really belonging to it; I can observe it at close quarters if I want to, but I don't have to engage with it.

In both cases there's a sense of being removed but connected at the same time, and in both cases I feel nourished by the humanity that flows around me as I write, as if I'm being borne along on the tide of life. It brings an odd feeling of completeness, a sense almost of inner homecoming, that seems very conducive to creativity. And to anyone who feels like trying it when next they have something to write, I would just say: spare a thought for those writers who weren't, or aren't, so lucky.

33 THINGS TO DO

If tomorrow you were locked up indefinitely with just a pencil and a single sheet of A4 paper, what would you write about to keep your sanity? Something very personal or something completely impersonal? Imagine yourself in a prison cell and try it.

Week 41
John to Jamie

HOME AND AWAY

It's homecoming for me this week, in a literal sense. I love travelling but I always love coming home. Last year, when we were running courses at Ty Newydd (the Welsh Writers' centre in Snowdonia), we worked with talented groups of bilingual Welsh writers. As ever my lack of foreign language skills left me yearning to be similarly fluent (in whatever language other than English), but I know it won't happen. What I did take away, though, was one Welsh word, suggested by one of the participants as her favourite. The word was *hiraeth*.

Hiraeth has a beautiful sound when spoken in Welsh. It means 'a longing for your native land' (English needs six words to define the one Welsh word). That Welsh should have such a word tells you much about Welsh sensibility and history. You start imagining and remembering the Welsh emigrant experience — the fact that there's a bit of Australia called New South Wales, or that there's a Welsh-speaking community in Patagonia at the bottom tip of South America.

As writers in English we need to remember that language has cultural roots. The understanding of particular words does not necessarily travel with the words themselves. Meaning shifts. So language evolves, and certainly English is now evolving in different parts of the world.

I say this particularly because a piece of work that I began in London a few months ago has now sprouted wings and is flying off to many different places in a 'global brand programme'. Colleagues from The Writer are this week running training sessions in Hong Kong, New York, Sao Paolo and Mumbai. They are training accountants and management consultants in the new tone of voice we have defined for PWC (PricewaterhouseCoopers). As with most multinational organisations, the operating language of the company is English.

There is always a debate in this situation. Do you tailor your approach to meet the more limited understanding of non-native English speakers? After all, clients will say, their people need to communicate simply and clearly using very few English words. Or do you say that English without nuance (a word borrowed from another language) is a language that loses its vital spark of life?

I veer towards the latter. Even a statement like this — 'Relationships create value' — can be unpacked in umpteen different ways by native and non-native speakers. That phrase was our starting point, and we laboured long and hard, going through countless drafts in meetings and committees to chew over each of the words and alternatives suggested. But the reality is that such statements will always be interpreted by the individual in a way that makes sense to that individual. Individuals will see it through the lens of their own language, culture and experience. It might be a distorting lens, but a managerial attitude of control freakery will create even more distortion. So, in the end, it depends on the ability of a trainer in workshops to educate, to draw out, as deep a shared understanding as possible in the individuals who make up the brand.

32 THINGS TO DO

Take one word, an abstract noun of your choice. Find its meaning in as many other languages as you can, using dictionaries, Google and speakers of that language. See how many possibilities there are, and see how many similarities there might be. Do you prefer the word in one of the other languages?

Jamie to John

TELLING TALES

And when the brand is you and you alone — as is the case for most people in that army of freelances and consultants who serve the corporate world — what then? What are *your* brand values? And if you've ever stopped to look at these values, how then do you communicate them? How do you let your clients know where you're coming from?

A couple of months ago, for the second year running, my wife and I went on a walking holiday in the Italian Alps with a couple who are among her oldest friends. Our relationship is that relative rarity — a foursome in which all members get on with each other equally well. Hughes is French and Caroline English, though she has lived in France for nearly four decades. My wife, Sarah, is of Scottish descent but was raised in the French Alps. She and Caroline are bilingual. Hughes' English has a certain idiosyncratic fluency all of its own. My French is the weakest link, though serviceable enough for most of our conversations to be conducted in an easy mix of both languages.

Our walks this year were punctuated by stops to photograph the glossy, docile cows that graze the high summer pastures, the soft clink of their bells offering an almost constant accompaniment to our Alpine rambles. An architect by profession, Hughes is also an artist who, as he approaches retirement from his architectural practice, is reacquainting himself with the easel by painting portraits of these delightful creatures.

But it's not his buildings or paintings that we talk about so much as his novels, for Hughes is also a novelist. And this is where we're limited by our respective linguistic skills, for neither of us is really able to read the other's work. So instead, we tell each other the stories of our books as we walk. This is a thoroughly companionable activity. It's also energising: rather as work songs help fishermen haul in their nets, so storytelling is a wonderful aid to tired legs. And it can be instructive: hearing oneself speak aloud a story of one's own creation throws its strengths and weaknesses into sharp relief.

But most of all it's personally revealing. We have probably learnt as much about one another from these fictions as we have from all the conversations we've had over the years. They have enriched an already cherished friendship because to tell a serious story is to engage with one's deepest human preoccupations; and whether we mean to or not, we lay ourselves bare in the telling of them.

Another way of saying that, of course, would be that we reveal our personal brand values. And this is the thing about stories, coming back to your point about language, John. Stories cut across all barriers of language because it's not the linguistic nuances but the human and universal in them — the things we understand whether we speak English, French, Japanese or Swahili — that make the true connections. They are, as we've both constantly reiterated in these pages, the ultimate connectors; and this is just as true whether you're a multinational corporation or a freelancer working out of your spare bedroom.

31 THINGS TO DO

What is your personal brand story? Give yourself an hour to write down the story you would tell a new client or colleague, or maybe feature on your website or professional network pages, to get across what you feel are the important things you stand for. It might be a true story, it might be made up. The important thing is that you believe in it and tell it in your own voice.

Week 42
John to Jamie

LEADING QUESTIONS

This week I'm in York running a writing workshop for the Leadership Foundation for Higher Education. Taking part are 15 senior academics from mainly British universities. I've run a dozen of these in the last few years but this latest one probably brings participants filled with greater anxiety and uncertainty than ever before. The university world is facing big changes, potentially catastrophic loss of funding, and these people will be on the frontline and needing to show leadership.

The Leadership Foundation has been enlightened in insisting that writing should be an important element of a broader course. My workshop is just one day out of three, but it's an intensive day in which the academics question their current writing style and move towards a different approach. The philosophy behind this is that you need to display leadership through words. And it's true that it's hard to think of an inspiring leader in business, politics or academic life who does not use words well.

The main problem is generally that writers for any large organisation seem to get stifled by their perception of the institution's size, importance and gravity. The result is dull, often impenetrable writing, characterised by long sentences with lots of sub-clauses, sending the reader in different directions, in which, like this sentence, it's all too easy to get lost. Keep it tight. Write shorter. Edit.

So we work through exercises involving compressed writing — short storytelling in many different forms. It comes down to constraints again: six-word stories, two-word sentences. It's interesting to observe what happens when you get people to complete a sentence with a single verb, having given them just an abstract noun as a starting point. Education, for example.

I recently had to take some of my own medicine. I'm on the board of the Poetry Society which, like many other organisations, is having to think clearly about what it is and what it stands for — the dreaded 'mission statement'. My heart sinks when I hear those words; most organisations see them as opportunities either for empty boasting ('To be Number 1') or for a baggy description of activities written with an eye on internal political tensions. The resulting position is neither missionary nor visionary.

The Poetry Society's starting point was too descriptive, listing impressive initiatives carried out to achieve the aim of spreading the word about poetry. I felt the statement needed to show the Society's leadership and ability to speak for poetry. It needed to be more about the potential of poetry and less about the Society's day-to-day activities. Here is the gist of it (the Arts Council form allowed 250 words):

> We're here to help poets and poetry thrive. Poetry comes in many forms from classical metre to the rhythm of rap, and increasingly it appears or is heard in different media. We champion poetry for people of all ages, backgrounds and personalities, helping them engage through the page, the internet and performance, making connections with people's lives and experiences.
>
> Poetry has enormous potential: to enrich, connect, entertain, transform, comfort and stimulate. Our mission is to help fulfil more of that potential.

These might not be the final words used. There could be fewer of them. But it comes back to the point that words show leadership and any organisation needs to answer the basic question: 'What are we in business for?'

30 THINGS TO DO
The shortest sentence in the Bible is 'Jesus wept'. Choose an organisation you're working with or in contact with. Write a succession of two-word sentences — noun plus verb — to describe that organisation's philosophy.

Jamie to John

INTO THE LIGHT

Last week the news was dominated by one of the year's most extraordinary, and certainly most uplifting, stories — the rescue of the 33 Chilean miners from their temporary tomb in the depths of the San José mine. As they emerged one-by-one from the hellish, 600-metre-long metal rescue tube, President Piñera, who had been on hand throughout with a seemingly inexhaustible supply of *bons mots*, declared that his country's most precious resource was not copper or gold, but 'we Chileans'.

It wasn't a particularly original sentiment, although in the circumstances it did have a very particular resonance. 'Our people are our most precious resource,' has become one of the tiredest of corporate clichés, trotted out daily by the unimaginative leaders of businesses and other organisations in every corner of the globe. Leaving aside the notion that people can be relegated to the status of mineral deposits, it's the 'our' — that possessive pronoun — that gives the game away. It implies something paternalistic, a little condescending, and it always carries an underlying sense of disconnection, as if the speaker and the people referred to don't belong to quite the same tribe.

But what made the President's declaration interesting was his choice of the word 'we'. It served to make the statement inclusive rather than exclusive. He included himself as one of the resources. 'We Chileans', he said. And in that moment, with that simple phrase, he summoned the image of a nation profoundly united.

As the miners were being winched to the surface, I was running a workshop for the internal communications department of a large financial institution in Edinburgh. I invited the participants to use art materials to portray where they felt their organisation was at present, and their unit within it. One group created an underwater scene complete with octopuses and sharks, shoals of small colourful fish, shipwrecks and a submarine. In the bottom left-hand corner was a blacked-out section, evidently a cave, from which peered several small, anxious pairs of eyes.

'Who's that in the cave?' I asked.

'Our leaders,' came the answer. 'They don't like to come out much.'

The kind of leaders, no doubt, who would be quick to proclaim that their people are their greatest resource, while failing to acknowledge that they themselves are part of the same rich seam of human talent and energy, emotion and intellect that keeps the business moving. And while this was obviously a source of frustration, even anger, for my group, I couldn't help feeling a pang of sympathy for those wretched leaders, failing to connect with the tribe they belonged to, trapped like the miners in their cave — though in this case not by a rockfall but by their own fear.

'You need to display leadership through words,' you said. Rethinking those business clichés that have become the white noise of our working lives is an excellent place to start — and perhaps to find some courage.

29 THINGS TO DO

List half-a-dozen of those business clichés that really set your teeth on edge. Then add another half-dozen from your own vocabulary, if you can — the ones you use without realising it. What do they really mean? Find alternative ways of saying them that give their meaning new life and fresh impact.

THE WRITER'S ART

We live in the world; and as writers you've just shown how, on an everyday level, we connect with the world's events. But, of course, it's a personal thing — we pick up on what interests us. The unusual aspect of the Chilean miners story was that it stirred such emotions around the entire world.

It's those universal emotions we need to connect with, though, and the best way to do so is, paradoxically, through personal experience. That thought lies behind this book and its title, *Room 121.*

It's also where 26 plays a distinctive role, enabling a group of business writers to connect the universal with the personal. We've just seen the culmination of our '26 Treasures' project that we referred to earlier. By this point in the year, I thought it might be in the past but it's still with us because the V&A likes the exhibition so much that they've extended it by a month.

For writers the most interesting part of the project could be not simply the final pieces, each of 62 words (a 'sestude'), but the stories behind the creation of the sestudes — a feat of concision. These 'creation stories' (no word limit) can be read on www.26treasures. com. Each creation story is individual; each writer went about the task in a different way.

You can read how, for example, a poet like Maura Dooley looked into her mirror and wrote. Or how a business strategist like Andy Hayes went on a long, uproarious journey that ended up in a sleazy bar in Inverness. Or how night thoughts came to copywriter John Fountain.

The message of these stories is not 'do it like this'. But you can read, think, adapt to your own way of working, and perhaps try something new. Because the one certain thing is that no writer should get stuck in a set way of thinking — there are always new things to learn. And there's no better way to learn than from other writers.

These thoughts were reinforced this week by the 26 annual speech, given this year by Howard Jacobson, who had just won the Booker Prize for *The Finkler Question*. It was a brilliant performance and here are some of his remarks that are worth thinking about.

We are all thin-skinned. As writers we want to remake the world. We take rejection personally.

Giving compliments that you have a gift for writing can actually give you that gift.

Without Thou shalt not commit adultery, adultery's not worth committing.

I like to take myself where I wouldn't normally go. This is the stuff of our humanity. Sex, belief, death. As a fiction writer I'm committed to uncertainty. I question everything.

I'm not interested in plot. But this is a story. Our being in this room, talking to each other.

He was talking about fiction but only a minor adaptation is needed to apply those thoughts to your own writing in other genres, including business writing.

28 THINGS TO DO

It's a good discipline. Take a project you're proud of. How did it come about? How did you first approach it? What was your starting point? What made it click in your mind? How did you work towards your final version? Write the 'creation story' describing how you wrote it.

BORED TO DISTRACTION

You talk about the apparent contradiction in the idea that it's personal experience that allows us to express universal emotions. In fact, much as though we each like to consider ourselves unique, so many of the experiences we have in our lives are common to everyone on the planet. Writing well — fiction or anything else — is mainly a matter of choosing the words that express the particular experience in as engaging and widely accessible way as possible.

So, good writing involves a degree of self-awareness, a willingness to put something of your personality into your words. 'That's all very well when it's marketing or direct mail,' people often say on workshops, 'but what about when it's something very factual and dry, a report or business plan or funding application, for example, that may even have to be written in the third person? What does personality mean then?'

The answer I usually give is: 'When did someone last ask you to rewrite something because it wasn't boring enough?' It's flippant, I know, and as often as not someone gives a wry smile and replies, 'You'd be surprised …' But I do believe that even the most stony-hearted bureaucrat, the most small-minded functionary, is not beyond the reach of conviction. Conviction, of course, is closely related to confidence (not to be confused with bumptiousness), neither of which is possible without a degree of self-awareness, and both of which are manifestations of personality.

Given the conviction, and the knowledge of your subject, it's perfectly possible to present facts or opinions on even the most technical matters in a strong, confident voice without resorting to management babble, corporate cliché or impenetrable abstraction. Even in the third person, that confidence represents personality, and the easiest way to display it is to use simple, direct language that wherever possible describes real people doing real things.

Below is an example we both use, from the annual report of Swedish telecoms giant Ericksson in the year they made the biggest loss in their country's corporate history:

2002 was tough.

Our customers bought less equipment, competition increased, the roll-out of 3G was slow, and the market was hard to predict.

Some observers see no end to these difficulties.

We take a very different view.

Confident as it sounds, on closer reading it becomes clear that it's actually more than a little disingenuous — 'Our customers bought less equipment'? How about, 'We sold less equipment'. But it does make the point about simplicity and (apparent) directness of language; and it's certainly the exception that proves the rule revealed by a survey of annual reports some years ago, which concluded that the length of chairmen's statements increased in direct proportion to the amount of trouble in which their companies found themselves.

Personality doesn't always have to mean a warm human voice or an obvious display of emotion, but it does, at the very least, mean a recognition that no one who is bored or bamboozled is really going to hear what you have to say.

27 THINGS TO DO

Take the Ericksson example and rewrite it in the densest business language you can. Make it long-winded, pompous and dull. Imagine a chairman who's trying their best to give the shareholders anything but the unvarnished truth. Then ask yourself, did it come easily? What did you learn from writing this way?

THINK ABOUT THE CHILDREN

It's not about getting older. I've always believed it's a duty, as a writer and a citizen, to do your best to help young people. You've written many novels for a younger audience, Jamie. The benefits of writing (and its associate activity, reading) start at a young age. Education — by which I mean 'drawing out' rather than target-setting and focusing on 'facts, facts, facts', Gradgrind style — needs to have writing at its core.

I've always done what I could in this area. Over 10 years I wrote thousands of words for Royal Mail's education programme. This centred around two products fundamental to Royal Mail's purpose: postage stamps and letter writing. Introducing Peter Firmin (creator of *The Clangers and Bagpuss*) at a recent event reminded me that some years ago I had written the words and Peter had produced the illustrations for Royal Mail's *Messages through the letterbox*. This was associated with a set of stamps based on characters from children's literature — from *Alice in Wonderland* to Peter's own *Noggin the Nog*. The booklet was distributed by Royal Mail to all UK primary schools. It was written for teachers and, through them, for school children. Looking at it again, 17 years on, the messages are ones I'm happy to stand by:

> *This book starts from the belief that if children enjoy writing, they will automatically become better at it. The book is designed to help children gain more enjoyment from writing, and therefore to improve their writing skills. There is nothing that opens up as many exciting possibilities, there is no more inspiring activity. There is no better game than writing.*

So when I opened up the Sunday paper and read this, it struck a chord with me. The film maker Beeban Kidron has founded a cinematic library project, making classic films available for after-school clubs. The evidence shows that it helps children perform better in the classroom. Why should that be so? Beeban Kidron answered:

I think that stories, and the telling of stories, are the foundations of human communication and understanding. If children all over the country are watching films, asking questions and telling their stories, then the world will eventually be a better place.

The latest stage of this story is that I have just written the website for the Ministry of Stories. Nick Hornby launched the 'Ministry of Stories' this week in a Monster Store in Hoxton High Street, east London. The idea is based on Dave Eggers' 826 Valencia that has been so successful in the US. The aim is to encourage young people to write imaginatively to tell stories in whatever form they wish. Volunteer writing mentors work with them at after-school workshops at the Ministry, behind the Monster Store. The writing — poems, stories, rap lyrics, comic strips — is digitally printed so that each child becomes an author.

It's a wonderful project and I enjoyed writing the website. It's important to do what we can for the next generation of writers.

26 THINGS TO DO

Here's an exercise taken from that Royal Mail book on letter writing. It was written for children but it applies to all of us — find the child inside you. 'Think back to yesterday. What did you do? Describe what kind of day it was and some of the things that you saw around you.'

READING BETWEEN THE LINES

Yes, as a visiting author I've spent a lot of time on my hind legs in front of classrooms full of teenagers. Apart from providing entertainment, giving the teachers a break, and maybe selling a few books, there's always the hope that I might kindle a spark of enthusiasm for reading or writing where previously there was none.

At first these school events used to terrify me. Then I came to realise two things: one, that for all the affectation of adolescent *ennui*, the kids are mostly dying to be engaged; and two, that almost no one is immune to the power of a good story. Which is not to say that mine are particularly good, but I choose passages that I hope will be gripping and make the reader work hard. There's a moment that I've come to know and love, when I see their eyes go dreamy and I know that I've got them; that for the next half hour or so they'll forget that they're 14 and that their lives depend on seeming cool.

Then we talk about stories — where they come from, how you create characters, how you build plot — and sometimes we do an exercise which is a variation on one you introduced me to years ago, John, and that we both use in our business workshops. It's a reading from a play called *Mnemonic* by the Theatre de Complicité, and it's about memory and imagination. It invites the audience to close their eyes and cast their minds back to various moments in their lives, one of which is their very first day at school. It asks them to picture the shoes they were wearing on that day. When the reading's over I get the kids to write a description of that first day, in the first person, as if they were the shoes. I've never yet met someone who couldn't do this exercise. Finally, they ask questions and there's one that always crops up: 'How did you become a writer?', to which I always give the same answer: 'I was a reader first.'

Today, as I sit here writing this, it strikes me how very little difference there is between the sessions I run for teenagers about fiction, and the sessions we run for adults about writing in business. The principles are exactly the same. We all have some kind of imagination, we all want to make connections. The trick is in putting the two together, whether you're a 14 year-old with a creative writing project or a chief executive with a business plan. And reading, being aware of how other people use language to tell stories, is possibly the best kind of instruction you can get.

Michael Foot, the former Labour Party leader, who died earlier this year, once said: 'The men who do not read are unfit for power'. My version of this would be: 'The men and women who do not read are unfit to communicate'. And yes, we do have a responsibility to the next generation of writers, part of which is to tell them: 'You can't start reading soon enough.'

25 THINGS TO DO

Here's another thinking-back exercise — this time to your very first day at work. But rather than from the perspective of the shoes you were wearing, write it from the viewpoint of a colleague or a boss. Who did they see turning up for work that day? What was their first impression of the new recruit?

Week 45
John to Jamie

TAKE NOTE

I always take two objects with me as travelling companions. The first is the book I happen to be reading at that time; reading a book as I travel between meetings in London is essential for me. Rather than reading for work, I find that reading a personal choice of book refreshes my mind and leaves me better prepared for whatever work I'm doing.

The second object is a notebook, generally a Moleskine (it has a good founding story, tucked into its back flap). For me the notebook is different from a daily journal. Some days I might not write in it at all. Generally I use it to make notes during meetings, recording real words used whenever possible. But I also use the notebook to jot down thoughts and ideas for current and future projects. It's a safe place to record thoughts because no one else sees them until I'm ready to show them.

I rarely show anybody the writing in the notebook because it's not ready yet. It's the first stage in the writing process. The next stage, for me, is typing up the words from the notebook to my computer. I can edit a little as I type, changing a word or a phrase, but further editing will be needed once I've printed out the writing I've just typed. So there are at least three stages of editing involved in each piece of writing. That's not excessive, and some writers are much more obsessive editors. I've often quoted David Ogilvy's remark: 'I'm a lousy copywriter but I am a good editor'. We all need to become better editors of our own work.

The notebook, though, is the essential part of all this, and the part I get most pleasure from. It's a reassuring presence in my pocket. Raw thoughts can grow into cooked ideas in the notebook. It's what works for me, but I know other writers have their own methods and habits. We all need to find the way that works best for us.

Here's a poem that was edited by award-winning poet Jen Hadfield at a Dark Angels course this year. She got each of us to write a couple of lines about writing and talking, each beginning, 'What I love/like'. Jen stitched these together, then we read the lines as a continuous poem in the group. I think of them as an extract from a collective notebook.

what i love about writing is the &
what i love about talking is no-one can tell i can't spell

what i love about writing is the sound of the pen scratching
the paper
what i love about talking is the silences which speak volumes

what i like about writing is the ability to stealth-bomb
what i like about talking is the opportunity to hear yourself

what i love about writing is the shape of the words
what i love about talking is the sound of the words

what i love about writing is the absence of sound
what i love about talking is the presence of sound

what i love about writing is thinking out quietly
what i love about talking is phosphorus and flint

what i love about writing is its dendrites
what i love about talking is you you and you

what i love about writing is the anticipation
what i love about talking is the inevitability

what i like about writing is i say what i mean
what i like about talking is people know what i mean

what i love about writing is what i find
what i love about talking is your thoughts

what i love about writing is it lies
what i love about talking is it flows

what i love about writing is its deep sea
what i love about talking is its tides

what i love about writing is its crusty edge
what i love about talking is its underbelly

24 THINGS TO DO

Add two lines of your own to the list of 'What I love
about writing/talking'. Where would you place your
couplet for best effect?

NICE HANDWRITING

I'm a convert to writing by hand, and you converted me to it. Something different happens when you set aside the keyboard and open a notebook. In fact, a lot of different things happen.

An attractive notebook has personality in a way that even the snazziest of laptops never will. Picking a clean page and sharpening a pencil, or twiddling open a propelling pencil, becomes a kind of ritual — rather like rolling a cigarette — that is pleasurable in itself. Then there's the feeling of the pencil in your fingers, the paper beneath your hand. And in my case, until I succumbed to the propelling variety, there was the little tin containing a rubber, sharpener and sometimes a pile of pencil shavings. The whole process is natural, organic and visible, and it continues to remind me of my childhood ambition to fill an empty notebook entirely with words. I never managed it, but it may be one of the reasons I became a writer.

There's another sense in which writing by hand is more organic. Until a few years ago I wrote my novels on screen, painstakingly editing as I went along, always striving for perfect meaning and the *mot juste*. They took me a long time. The first four averaged five years apiece. Then came a minor success, and the need for a follow-up in somewhat shorter order. I ditched the computer, bought notebooks and pencils, and wrote the first draft by hand straight off in nine months. The physical head-hand connection, the feeling that I was literally drawing the story out of myself with the movement of my pencil across the paper, made the story faster and more fluent; and to my great surprise the end result needed relatively little editing. It wasn't necessarily a better book than its predecessor but it was tighter, it had more energy and, I like to think, no less depth.

In our workshops we encourage people to write by hand. We want them to reconnect with this more natural process. We invite them to 'sidestep the inner policemen' as the former poet laureate, Ted Hughes, used to call the business of bypassing our critical selves and getting straight to that deeper place where our real creative resources lie.

With the students we tend to do short bursts of this kind of writing — three to five minutes at a time. But there's a longer version which serves not only to exercise the writing muscle, but can also offer valuable personal insights. This is the daily journal, except that it's not a journal in the conventional sense of being a chronological record of events, but more of a private daily visit to the subconscious.

A few years ago I kept one of these daily journals for a period of about nine months. I wrote for half-an-hour first thing every morning, by hand, pausing as little as possible, about whatever came into my head. I used to cover between two and three ruled A4 pages. It helped me with two very important things. I began to hear my own writer's voice very clearly, and I became much clearer in my thinking about a number of issues I had previously found confusing. It took a while to start working, but after a few months I began to feel that I was responding to some deeper pulse I had not previously been aware of. On one occasion I found myself witnessing and describing what I can only assume was my own creative source — a small spring of perfectly pure, clear water welling up at the bottom of a dark cave. It was an image I'll carry with me for the rest of my life.

23 THINGS TO DO

Try writing your own daily journal. Just aim for 10 minutes a day to start with — that should be about one side of A4. Start with whatever happens to be on your mind when you sit down and allow the thoughts to take you where they will. It's for your eyes only.

Week 46
John to Jamie

IT'S A SIN

Perhaps technology encourages pride? There's a natural humility that goes with writing by hand in a notebook. Whereas the power of modern mobile communications puffs up personal pride.

This struck me particularly when I was watching the reality TV show, *The Apprentice*, and observing those contestants with their ostentatious gadgets. I find the series strangely compelling but I really don't believe it has much to do with succeeding in the real business world. As usual Alan (Sir/Lord) Sugar, not necessarily the world's greatest businessman, gathered in a motley collection of would-be wheeler-dealers, attracted by the lure of a £100,000-a-year job. You get to know the participants on camera through the tasks they're set, and through their words: 'Everything I touch turns to sold'. Their overweening pride has to be heard to be believed: 'There's nothing mediocre about me'; 'I'm at the top of my game'; 'I'll always give you 110%'.

A few weeks ago we were both in Spain for our latest Dark Angels course. One of our exercises is to set people to write a typical corporate piece in the tone of voice of one of the seven deadly sins — gluttony, envy, etc. This time, more than ever, it became clear that pride is *the* corporate sin. It's the default tone of the corporation.

I hadn't expected to get such a quick confirmation of this when, after the course, I stayed at a hotel in the old quarter of Seville. It was a lovely-looking hotel, a labyrinth of plants, paths and patios between the rooms. But behind the attractive façade, there were a lot of services that didn't function all that well: plumbing, TV, wi-fi, drinks in the bar. The hotel's directory of services didn't go in for modesty. They told me that they had a vision: 'Above the stars'. They also had a mission:

It is our aim to achieve economic yield that allows us to improve, innovate and expand the services that we offer every day, as well as carry out our projects.

They concluded like this:

Our professional staff is always available to make sure that you have an unforgettable stay. For the exceptional character of our buildings and the professional service we offer our guests, we like to think that our hotels are beyond the stars.

Look on your words, you mighty corporations, and despair. If you can't take my order for a glass of red wine in less than half an hour, your pride is empty, and so is my glass. Pride is the most prevalent corporate sin and it's described even more powerfully in its Spanish form — *vanagloria*. It's as straightforward as this: if business writing is less vainglorious, it will be more effective.

22 THINGS TO DO

Choose a 'deadly' sin: pride, gluttony, lust, avarice, envy, anger or sloth. Now choose a company that proclaims exceptional focus on customer service. Rewrite one of that company's paragraphs in the tone of the sin that you have chosen. It's a good antidote to the temptation of over-claiming.

Jamie to John

ORAL HYGIENE

… And *vanagloria*, as we all know, comes before a fall — perhaps nowhere more spectacularly than in the case of RBS (Royal Bank of Scotland), the architect of whose collapse, Fred Goodwin, I once had the disagreeable task of interviewing for an annual report. He was running a different bank in those days. Halfway through our interview he hauled in a senior executive and gave him a dressing down in front of me. After that I followed his career with a certain grim curiosity and, I have to admit, raised a cheer when, a decade or so later, he finally fell from grace.

'Make It Happen' and 'Enjoy Better Banking With RBS' were two of Royal Bank of Scotland's pre-crash slogans — both of which would seem highly ironic today. Now it claims a little more humbly, and quite literally since we taxpayers own half of it, to be 'Here for you'. A quick trawl of other websites reveals that its cousin, Bank of Scotland, is companionably 'With you all the way', while Lloyds TSB wants you to know that it's 'For the journey'. What, like a ham sandwich? NatWest prides itself on offering 'Helpful banking' (try applying the principle of opposites, NatWest), while HSBC modestly considers itself 'The world's local bank'. My own, the Clydesdale, is 'Always thinking' — I would be intrigued to know about what. Only Barclays, wisely in my view, says nothing.

Of course financial services organisations are easy targets, particularly in the current climate. But even now they still seem to suffer more than most from *vanagloria* — emphasis on the *vana* since so many of the claims they make are so patently empty once you examine the reality of their service. Part of the problem, however, and it's not confined to the world of financial services, is the corporate urge to describe a business in three or four words. I've never really understood it, because it's such a difficult thing to do; the results are so often fatuous or vacuous, and they almost always become hostages to fortune.

Which is where the paradox lies, because however inane they may sound, they're also powerful, those innocuous little words, and when things go wrong and people hold them against you, they can do great damage. So you have to use them carefully and, most importantly, truthfully. Claim to be 'With you all the way', then demand that a struggling small business repays its overdraft, and the words develop a septic tinge. Much better not to try at all and just keep your own counsel, like Barclays.

As the playwright Dennis Potter once famously said:

The trouble with words is that you never know whose mouths they've been in.

'Or are going to end up in,' I would add.

21 THINGS TO DO

Take a business or brand you know well and write the shortest possible meaningful statement of what you think it's about. How many words does it take you?

Week 47
John to Jamie

A SPIRIT OF GENEROSITY

I'd like to turn from sin to virtue. That doesn't really mean I'm thinking of redemption and repentance. I believe it's important that we give something back to people, places and activities that have nurtured us, to do what we can to help others gain from our experience. Hence this book. Hence our training activities.

This week I've started writing for the National Theatre again. Ten years ago, while at Interbrand, I'd led the team that looked afresh at the National Theatre brand. That had been a labour of love for me because the National Theatre has been an important part of my life since my teenage years. As part of that work I'd written a long report about what the National is, what it stands for and how it achieves its aims — foolishly ambitious in that it consumed solid weeks of my time. The fact was that I felt a heavy responsibility to do the best I could for this wonderful institution that had given me so much. It was still daunting to go and present the report to the board with much-admired writers like Ben Okri and Tom Stoppard sitting around the table reading my words.

Ten years on and they've invited me back to 'write their

story' for a major fundraising project, NT Future. They aim to raise £70 million over the next couple of years. I began my task with interviews, looking at architectural models and reading documents. In that research material I came across this phrase: 'A spirit of generosity informed the founding of the National'.

I liked that phrase, and I believe we should all have a spirit of generosity because it makes us better writers. Why so? Because you need empathy, you need to imagine the thoughts and feelings of others to write well, and you cannot do that if you approach writing in a mean-spirited way.

I guess I'm also saying that *Room 121*, where you share thoughts as a writer with a reader, is a room of generosity. But the room demands honesty and openness to support that generosity.

Here's part of the introduction I've just written for the National:

The building changes enable us to reshape positively the relationships between all those involved in our community: actors, audiences, directors, writers, other theatres, craftspeople, educators, academics, young people, teachers, lifelong learners, visitors. The local, national and international. Those with advantages and those without. The persuaded and the persuadable. The fanatical and the sceptical, those waiting on the doorstep, those just passing by.

Everyone.

To achieve our long-held belief that theatre is for everyone. The National Theatre can lead the world in demonstrating how that is so.

20 THINGS TO DO

Which institution (school, museum, university?) has meant most to you in your life? Have you ever written about that institution's influence on you, and the way it shaped you? Take half an hour to do that, being open and honest with yourself. You might be surprised at the emotion released through writing.

A CLOSE ENCOUNTER

Earlier this year I visited an institution of a very different sort. I mention it because the visit entailed a 'giving back' of the kind you describe. What I was quite unprepared for was what I got out of it in return.

If I had been asked as they filed in to point out the one that most unnerved me, it would have been him. Thick set, bull-headed and covered with tattoos, he had a penetrating stare and a menacing energy. Several of the prisoners, I had been warned, were on methadone, and that made them dopey; but this character wasn't dopey, he was wired. I explained that I was going to talk about and read from my own books, and then we were going to do some exercises. 'Let's keep it informal,' I added. 'If you want to ask questions as we go along, that's fine.'

We were in one of the visiting rooms, an upstairs space the size of a tennis court, with comfortable seating and spectacular views over coils of razor wire to the nearby hills; 17 long- and medium-term prisoners, the writer-in-residence, half a dozen sceptical prison officers who, for the time being, were keeping their distance, and me.

I had hardly finished my introduction when Tattoos asked his first question. He didn't so much ask it as fire it at me, a staccato burst of almost unintelligible local patois. I had to wait while my brain decoded what it had heard before I could answer him. Three minutes later there was another burst. And so it continued for nearly two hours. Every time I paused, and sometimes when I didn't, Tattoos had another question. They were smart questions: about research, about characterisation and the role of personal experience in the writing process, about what is fiction and what isn't.

I could feel my prejudices being dismantled. This was a curious, intelligent person, albeit one who severely lacked an education and had doubtless been let down by both society and himself in other ways. But his hunger to learn was insatiable, and so was his desire to express himself. We ended with an exercise I have always loved, where people are given a series of prompts to describe someone they know using only metaphors. The result is a poem which brings the subjects alive in a vivid, unexpected and often emotionally charged way.

'Who would like to share what they've written with us?' I asked, fully expecting lowered eyes and an embarrassed shuffling of feet. But Tattoos had his hand up almost before I'd finished asking. I nodded and he fired off his poem as he had done the questions, at high speed, from somewhere at the back of his throat. It was good. He'd chosen the prison governor as his subject and it was funny and heartfelt, ironic as well as poignant. 'You are the Gucci watch of the Scottish Prison Service,' was the opening line. If he'd read it slowly enough for everyone to hear, he would have got a big laugh.

Even so, when he'd finished there were general murmurings of appreciation and I congratulated him fulsomely. His face widened in a beam of the most childlike pleasure. At the time I had no idea what he was in for, but I wondered when anyone had last told him he'd made a good job of something. Later I learnt that he had been a gangland hitman. He was a multiple murderer. It didn't stop me carrying that smile inside me like a charge of raw solar energy.

19 THINGS TO DO

Can you think of an encounter with someone that has changed the way you think about things? Write an account of that encounter. Describe as much of the detail as you can remember, including the feelings you experienced at the time and after.

STILL LEARNING

Your last piece shows that we never stop learning, Jamie. An uncomfortable experience but it certainly made an impression. We have to keep learning to keep our own performance high, to constantly challenge ourselves to get better at what we do.

For me, D&AD helps. This is the leading organisation for 'the creative industries' (by which it means design and advertising). D&AD is a charity, and it does educational work, aiming to achieve excellence in the industries it represents. I run workshops for them and have often served on the 'Writing for design' jury for the D&AD awards (winners receive a Yellow Pencil, the equivalent of an Oscar).

I was foreman of the jury this year and this week chaired a panel of fellow jurors and award-winners at a D&AD event. We gathered in a crowded room in the former Truman's Brewery off Brick Lane, to share thoughts on what makes great writing. I'd asked each of the panellists to talk about an example of their own work and an example of someone else's work. For my own part I talked about '26 Treasures' and an example from David Ogilvy, one of the great advertising writers of last century.

I've learnt a lot from David Ogilvy. Reading his books many years ago confirmed me as a writer (rather than a manager) but also confirmed writing as an essential skill for management. You need it to get on. For example, this was the first Ogilvy quote I selected for one of my books:

> *If everybody in our company took an exam in writing, the highest marks would go to the 14 directors. The better you write the higher you go in Ogilvy & Mather. People who think well, write well.*

But there was a further message to help you become a better manager. David Ogilvy says, perhaps not in such mundane words, that people matter. Unless you learn to manage people, you won't manage at all. And part of that approach to people management is that you should set your expectations high. If you have high expectations of people, they are more likely to perform than if you expect very little of them.

Obvious, perhaps. But Ogilvy really meant it. He once advertised for a creative director: 'Wanted: Trumpeter Swan'. The Trumpeter Swan is a rare bird indeed. But why settle for less?

This made him a hard taskmaster and people lived in some trepidation of what he might say about them. But generally they responded positively. Ogilvy & Mather became (and still is) one of the world's leading advertising and marketing companies. Working for Ogilvy might often have been an uncomfortable experience but you would never be in doubt that he wanted you to care. He wanted you to care as much as he did.

Once, he sent a memo about future creative directors.

Eleven of you told me that you have nobody who could qualify. You have problems. Something wrong with your hiring methods? Ten of you have not answered. Bastards.

Not settling for the mediocre, always expecting the highest standards, is a quality shown by many managers. I've worked for many who were like that — and I stuck with them. And it's a quality lacked by many managers of companies I was only too happy to leave.

18 THINGS TO DO

Choose your own examples: a piece of work you're proud of and an example of work you admire. Why have you chosen them? Write 500 words to explain and reveal something to yourself about yourself.

Jamie to John

BIRDS OF A FEATHER

As we near the end of the book I think about the things that I haven't yet written about, yet which are important to me. Your involvement with D&AD has obviously been significant in your working life. I agree that having to think about other people's work, whether as judge, reviewer or teacher — and like you, I've been all three — requires that you look very hard at your own practice. If we're talking about standards, this is something that definitely encourages you to up your own game.

My version of D&AD would probably be the Edinburgh International Book Festival. My good fortune is to sit on the board, which I have done now for a decade — although what I get out of it is something slightly different. This is what our website says:

> We are the largest public celebration of books in the world.
> Every August Edinburgh International Book Festival brings
> writers and thinkers from across the planet together to rub
> shoulders with you, the audience.

Naturally, I'm proud to be part of that. Seven hundred events and a quarter of a million visitors over 17 days represents a powerful amount of writing, reading, talking, listening and thinking. But this isn't a commercial for the festival... More than anything else, my involvement with it brings me a sense of community, of belonging. And that's important because writers tend not to be professionally gregarious and much of the time our work is solitary.

At a fairly basic level we just need the human contact; there have been times when I've been deep in a writing project and have ended up longing for someone to invite me to a meeting — about anything at all. But more than that it's the community of interest that we need because it validates our own choices, thoughts and feelings.

Over the years I've shared a stage with some very big literary names. My job is to be as transparent as possible, to make them feel comfortable and provide them with the best platform for what they have to say. One of the things that makes this possible is the knowledge that whoever they are we will always have certain essential things in common: a love of words and language and a desire to get at the truth of what we write about.

In the literary world this is a given. In the business world, less so. One is likely to feel more alone as a writer of serious intent working in or for large organisations where those things are not valued, or at least not acknowledged, in the same way. I'm sure this is what you had in mind, John, when you founded 26. It's certainly one of the things we've wanted to achieve with this book: to let people know that there *is* a community of writers out there working in the business world, people who set store by exactly the same fundamentals as those big literary names, people who want their words not simply to serve their clients' needs, but to make a difference wherever they can. We are both part of that community and we hope that perhaps you are too, dear reader.

17 THINGS TO DO

This may seem obvious, and it's certainly an unashamed commercial, but visit the website of 26 (www.26.org.uk) and see the kind of writers who flock together under that banner.

Week 49
John to Jamie

THE POWER OF COLLABORATION

Recently I've been thinking a lot about the subject you've just raised. The reason is that I've been asked to give a lecture at Falmouth University early in the new year. The audience will be students of writing, advertising and design, and members of the creative business community in Cornwall.

Talking to Tom Scott from Falmouth, the lecturer who invited me, we decided that I should talk about the power of creative collaboration. He wants the student writers and designers to work more closely together. As it happens there is a new 26 project that will do just that. It's called '26 Flavours' and will celebrate Cornwall's food and drink. There's much more to celebrate than the pasty, but I love the fact that the Cornish pasty came out of local working life. It was the lunch that miners took down into the mines, a complete meal, almost in its own pastry casing lunchbox.

I sat down this week to write my lecture. I'm calling it 'The writer and the world'. For me, openings are always important so I felt I was under way, with a clear direction ahead, when I wrote these first words:

> *Once you could tell the writer.*
> *He or she was the one not in the room.*
> *Writers were a shy, retiring bunch, and they didn't get out much. Most of the time, like me, they worked in various agencies and called themselves by any name other than 'writer'. You just seemed more likely to be doing a valued job if you called yourself a project manager, strategist or business head. Then you could fit in the bits of the job you really enjoyed — the writing — around the creation of charts, tables and figures.*

The fact is, if you write, you do much more than just put words down; you're not simply filling the spaces between images. You're thinking for the client who pays you, you're helping that business to solve problems. You just happen to concentrate on the most powerful way to think — by using words.

But words aren't used in isolation. They're even more powerful when you combine them with images, and I enjoy working with designers and visual artists. That's what I've done throughout my career. I enjoy the collaborative process between a writer and a designer, where the writer's words can generate imagery, and the designer's visual thinking can release words from the writer's imagination.

So I'm building up examples for Falmouth. I now realise that in recent years I've been working more and more collaboratively, and 26 has been the impetus for this. Through 26, hundreds of writers have become more creatively engaged with the world. Projects have involved working with organisations as diverse as the British Library, the Scotch Malt Whisky Society, London Underground, International PEN and the V&A. Each project has enriched the lives and working practices of the writers involved, but also the designers, curators, marketing managers, tube staff, manufacturers and other working people who have been involved in the collaborations.

In a sense it takes me back to that spirit of generosity I wrote about a little while ago. You give something out, you get something back. Collaboration demands a generous spirit but it repays generosity with generosity.

16 THINGS TO DO

For your next writing task, you're denied the use of words. Your task might be a speech, a report or a website. Map out what you need to say as a storyboard, using only pictures. Don't make the excuse 'I can't draw' — it's only you who will see the drawings.

Jamie to John

A DISAPPOINTMENT

For the last 10 days now we've been blanketed with snow. Not the usual soggy British stuff, but dry powdery Arctic snow, and the temperature continues to plummet. It was -12°C here last night, -15°C predicted for tonight. The coldest December on record, they're saying already. Against this frozen backdrop, a memory of sun and warmth has been whispering at me insistently, and your talk of collaboration has given me the cue to write about it.

A few years ago now, one of those once-in-a-career jobs came my way. I was invited to spend three weeks in Cognac, France, to write a small promotional book for Rémy Martin. It was to be a beautifully produced and illustrated collection of stories about the spirit and the company. It would be given away with every bottle of a new super luxury cognac, retailing at around £1500 per bottle and aimed at black American rappers, Japanese businessmen and the Russian nouveau riche.

I travelled out with the creative director and photographer from The Big Picture, a small Aberdeen-based brand agency with a big reputation in the whisky industry. One of Rémy Martin's brand ambassadors looked after us as we toured the rich, rolling Cognac region, visiting vineyards, warehouses, distilleries and cooperages, interviewing foresters and wine-growers, chemists, master-blenders and marketing directors, immersing ourselves in the history of the company and the business of making cognac.

Then the agency team went home and left me to carry on researching and start writing. Rémy Martin had been founded in 1722, but something of the place, the *terroir* — as the French call that indefinable relationship between landscape, soil, climate and vine — had got under my skin and was telling me I needed to start the story earlier than that. Cognac is at the heart of the Charente region, occupied by the Romans more than 2000 years ago. With its distinctively chalky soil, the invaders knew at once that this would be a good place to plant the vines they had brought with them. And there I had my opening:

> *Once long ago, a great sea covered all of France. Warm and shallow, it teemed with life. Vast ancestral fishes swam in its waters. Myriads of crustaceans and molluscs swarmed in its depths. Corals and sponges grew in profusion on its reefs. Plankton and algae and other microscopic creatures without number drifted through the tepid brine. As they died they settled on the sea-bed like a constant shower of dust.*

Over the aeons the continents rearranged themselves and new lands began to emerge. France shrugged off the sea and felt her earth warming in the sunlight. In places the soil was rich with the shells and skeletons of countless tiny marine organisms. Pale and porous, this was chalk.

On the facing page was a beautiful fully-bled photograph of pale, friable chalk soil in which nestled two perfect white ammonites.

The book went on to unfold in a series of similar miniature chapters, each illustrated with stunning images. Even before I had finished writing it I knew it was going to be one of those projects that I would always be truly proud to have been part of. The shared vision of several people across two countries was being spectacularly realised.

And then came the blow. The product launch had been shelved. In the end our beautiful little book never saw the light of day. I still have a bound proof copy on my desk and dip into it from time to time for the memories and, I admit, for the pleasure of the words and images. Had I not had my collaborators to commiserate with, it would have been much harder to swallow. The only lesson from this was that sometimes one has to be satisfied with a job well done even if almost no one else knows of its existence. Then it must be enough to know that one has given it everything one could.

15 THINGS TO DO

Origins are a good place to start stories. I don't mean founding stories but stories that might spring from the raw materials from which something is made. Think of a product you admire. What is it made from? Tell the story of the material or materials and see what metaphors they offer for the brand itself.

THERE IS A SEASON

One difference between us as writers is that my natural habitat is the city whereas yours is the countryside. It gives our business writing slightly different slants. Your starting point for Rémy Martin was making the connection between *terroir*, the origins of the earth and the potency of the drink. When I was meeting a similar challenge for Guinness, my starting point was on the barricades with Arthur Guinness as he resisted Dublin city officials.

Our origins shape us, sending our writing in different directions. But there are natural cycles that all of us share, in city or country, and I always enjoy using these in my writing for business. They're a way of connecting to a universal pool of thoughts and feelings that we all draw from.

This week I've been writing seasonal words for one client and observing them for another. The writing has been for a brand called Ila that I've worked with since its creation by Denise Leicester four years ago. Denise has an air of gentleness and spirituality. To source her spa and aromatherapy products, she tracks down ingredients in remote parts of the world, working in partnership with local people: Berber women in Morocco, Kashmiri tribespeople, natives of the Amazonian rainforest.

This week I've been writing about a new product development that links treatments to the natural rhythms of the body through the changing seasons. I called the approach 'Four seasons of stillness' and wrote this opening paragraph as part of Ila's presentation to John Lewis:

> *Life has a natural rhythm. The sun rises and falls. The tide ebbs and flows. Spring follows winter, summer fades into autumn. Your body moves to the beat of your heart. Listen to your breathing.*

Deep inside every woman there is a natural stillness,
an inner peace from which modern life too often disconnects
us. This stillness is a quiet but powerful rhythm, an energy
that women can reconnect to and restore harmony within.
Four seasons of stillness expresses the Ila philosophy. We aim
to put your body in harmony with the natural progression
of the seasons throughout the year, finding points of stillness
in each.

Working with Ila challenges my urban cynicism, but I respect Denise's ethereal integrity. My words try to bridge the gap between idealism and commercial reality. Sometimes I look at what I've written and can't quite believe it was me.

At the same time I've been visiting House of Fraser department stores because they've asked me to advise on their tone of voice. This is inescapably the commercial world, influenced at this time by a completely different approach to the seasons. It's Christmas, and the signs in the store are all about 'buy buy buy'. Actually, at this time of financial austerity, there are more numbers than words as you look around: '20% off', '30%', '50%' is the instore panorama facing customers. I fill my notebook with words and thoughts, storing them away like those seasonal foods we enjoy in the depths of winter. They'll take on a new life when I look at them again in the new year.

14 THINGS TO DO

At what time of year are you reading this? Write a paragraph or two about this particular season. What are the images, rhythms and moods of the season? If you were a retailer — choose one you work with or shop in — how could you use what you have written for a seasonal promotion?

COUNTRY MATTERS

Although I lived in London from the ages of roughly 20 to 40, I've lived in the country for twice as long, and you're right to say that it's my natural habitat. I'm perfectly at ease in the city but I'm really *at home* in the country, particularly on the edge of the Scottish Highlands, where I've lived for the last 20 years. The connection with land and landscape is deep in my bones, a source of both inspiration and comfort; and I notice more and more that at the slightest opportunity it surfaces in what I write.

I also think that this connection serves to soften what I write and perhaps encourages me to put more heart into my words. Which is not to suggest that you must live in the country to write with conviction or passion — you're living proof of the contrary, John — but perhaps that the further away you get from it (and here I picture not only inner city office blocks but outer-ring business parks), the further you are from one of the things that links us profoundly as humans; one of the things that creates the 'kindness' I have spoken about elsewhere and that I believe is so important to the way we communicate. Perhaps, in my earlier list of the sources of modern business-speak, I should have included alienation from the natural world.

If it sounds here that I'm advocating the 'Bambification' of business writing, I'm not. There are any number of subjects, including — increasingly — the natural world itself, that may need to be written about in a dispassionate manner. But to read, say, an environmental sustainability report whose author appears to be disconnected from his or her subject is to experience a basic failure of communication. And this, tragically, characterises so much of the language of the 21st century workplace.

It's not that we need to describe the forest or reed-bed in emotional terms, or with the lyricism of your Ila presentation, but rather that there is a natural flow to the language in which we present the facts or make the case. No matter what the subject, nor how objective we purport to be, we must still be able to tap into, as you say, that 'universal pool of thoughts and feelings that we all draw from.' And our connection with the natural world has a central place in that universal pool. To say otherwise is to suggest that the moon is made of *manchego*.

The natural world is there not so much to inspire us in what we write, but in who we are; to help us become properly joined-up — head, heart and hand — in the way we express ourselves. I find myself in my natural surroundings, and that makes me a better writer. It also makes me a better husband, father, grandfather and many other things besides.

13 THINGS TO DO

What draws us to particular places? Choose a favourite outdoor location — it might be somewhere you've visited on holiday, somewhere near where you live, or maybe even a city park, and write about the connection you feel with it. Try and get below the surface. Why do you like that copse, that bend in the stream, that grassy bank so much?

Week 51

John to Jamie

DINING OUT ON STORIES

The year's coming to an end, which means the book is too. Next week, moving into a new year, we can look back and draw some conclusions from a year's exchanges. But, for now, Christmas is done and I've flown out of the country for a break.

I find myself in Berlin, a refugee from the big freeze in England. There's a mistake. It's -10°C in Berlin and the snow is a foot deep. But I'm here because six months ago, as I mentioned in *Week 17*, I went to Turkey and visited, among many other sites, the remains of the ancient Greek city of Pergamon. (My first full-time job was working for Robert Maxwell's Pergamon Press in Oxford, but that's another story.)

Anyway, while standing in the summer heat, and listening to the guide bemoan the fact that German archaeologists had looted the place of its treasures in the 19th century, the idea had been obvious. 'If you now want to see what Pergamon was like, you have to go to Berlin.'

That's why we stood queuing for an hour, in the coldest temperature I've ever experienced, outside the Pergamon Museum in Berlin. I've never been so frozen and never felt so relieved to come in from the cold.

The reconstruction of the Pergamon altar is astonishing. Vast fragments of sculpture, but much of it well-preserved; fragments of lettering too, in Greek, words from the past still trying to explain themselves today. But then it's time for late lunch after the museum. On the way we'd passed the Willy Brandt Institute, which had posed the question in its window 'Was ist Deutschland?' They'd answered with an alphabetical list, and I'd remembered that *Curry Wurst* had been chose to represent the letter C as a sign of modern German identity.

Have you ever had *Curry Wurst?* I hadn't either. Now was the time. Still feeling frozen through, a hot sausage covered in hot curry sauce was the surprisingly good lunch I needed.

I'm on a break for a few days but I can't cut off from writing; my notebook and pencil are in my pocket. Someone contacted me on my BlackBerry to ask: 'You're so busy. How on earth do you find the time to write about your life as well as live it?' I replied: 'I suppose because I think of my life as writing.' It seemed the right moment to write the ending for the Falmouth talk I'm delivering early in the new year. It goes like this:

> *Every day is full of storytelling moments. Stories are not the special province of writers: we all tell stories, it's what makes us human. But to be a good writer you need to tell stories well. You need to connect with the universal emotions we all*

feel and if you make that connection your stories and your words will have enormous power. You need to connect with the world, and you need to see that the writer's role is to make connections, to make sense of things, and to make the world we live in a better world.

12 THINGS TO DO

If Curry Wurst is now an element of German identity, what food do you feel most sums up your own personal identity? Why? Write about that food, telling yourself why it means so much to you.

Jamie to John

SKATING BACKWARDS

While you've been shivering in the pursuit of antiquity, I'm basking in a minor thaw — it's a mere -5°C today — and wondering what to do about a leaking central heating boiler. Though if we have to forego baths and warm ourselves at the log fire for a couple of days it will be nothing compared to the winter of 1963 when, I'm told, we had no running water in the house for several weeks. But I don't remember the miseries of that winter, just the fun. I was 14, home from boarding school, and most of Scotland was a vast winter playground.

There was endless tobogganing. The best, in front of a local 'big hoose', was down a long, very steep field and straight out across several hundred yards of frozen ornamental loch, dodging skaters, a motorbike (how it stayed upright I have no idea) and even a couple of cars. It was surely the dream toboggan run, the best thing outside the Cresta.

Then there was ice hockey. A neighbour had flooded a field to make a flight pond. Set in a hollow between two hills, it was shallow and froze very quickly. That winter it was a couple of acres of pure glass. We played with walking sticks and a shoe polish tin filled with sand to give it weight. God, could we skate — flat out across the ice, whacking the puck and occasionally each other, twisting and turning on sixpences until the surface was scored and powdered by our blades and our cheeks were crimson and burning with cold. Late in the afternoon the sky would turn pink and fill with skeins of geese heading down to the river to roost. I remember feelings of extreme exhilaration at the sport and the speed of it, combined with something close to awe at the beauty of our surroundings.

But the thing I remember best was skating backwards. I got good at it, skating forwards as fast as I could, then pivoting on one toe to whip round into the backwards movement with almost no loss of speed. Skating backwards involved making a snakelike movement of the hips as you transferred your weight from one ankle to the other; it seemed to depend on a good rhythm even more than skating forwards. If you got it right it was almost like flying. If you didn't you were liable to crack your skull.

It was only possible, in fact, if you were in a state of complete surrender to yourself, your limbs co-ordinated, your sense of spatial awareness keen, your heart strong and trusting in the inner gyroscope that would keep you upright and going in the right direction. It strikes me now that the moment when all these things come together is echoed in the moment you discover your writer's voice — which is only as much about having a good grasp of language as skating backwards is about having flexible ankles.

Writing is a way of being — and being in the moment. It's a lens through which we can see the world and reflect it back to others. Keeping the lens clean and clear means having all our faculties in play, all the time. We are writers not just in our minds and the tips of our fingers, but in our hearts and souls. We are writers in our desire to reflect the world faithfully and truthfully. We are writers in our wish to live in that world as authentically as we can. As writers we are skaters on the ice of life and our blades are words. When we are truly at one with ourselves, those words make us fly.

11 THINGS TO DO

Do you take part in sport or any other kind of outdoor activity? Next time you do, try and keep mental notes while you're doing it, even if it's just walking. Then write about the experience as deeply as you can: what skills did you use, what thoughts and feelings did you have, what muscles did you use? See what this sketch might tell you about other aspects of your life.

Week 52

We've reached the 52nd week, a conclusion to our year of exchanges. We've decided to write this final exchange as 10 pieces of concluding advice, five from each of us. Oh, and in the spirit of Room 121, we decided that each piece should be exactly 121 words.

OUR CLOSER FOR 10

WELCOME CONSTRAINTS. Some forms of writing come with more obvious forms of constraint than others. Poetry has constraints of lines, sometimes of metre, alliteration, rhymes. Business writing seems to contain few. Perhaps that's the problem. Constraints tighten your writing, they help liberate it from the shackles of 'the accepted'. Try pushing the boundaries. The 121 things to do are exercises based on constraints. Try as many of them as you can; they are for you. The advantages of these constraints is that they free you from everyday restrictions — the need to please someone else. Learn to satisfy your own writing principles, then it will be easier in time to please other readers. How so? Because writing is a matter of confidence.

10 THINGS TO DO

It's time for you to sum up the lessons of your reading. What advice would you now give yourself about becoming a better writer? Write that advice in exactly 121 words.

DEVELOP PERSONALITY. Putting more personality into what you write has become a mantra for both of us. 'But what exactly do you mean by that?' we are frequently asked in workshops. Try the principle of opposites, is one reply. What would happen if you put less personality into what you write? The result would be words that are impersonal, the kind we so often hear from large organisations, the kind that don't make any real connection with us as readers. More personality doesn't necessarily mean words that sing with your individual voice. It simply means that when you hear them they sound as if they've been written by another human being, probably much like you. It's easy to spot the difference.

9 THINGS TO DO

Find the most turgid, lifeless piece of business writing you can. Put it into the first person, probably plural. Replace the nouns with verbs. Make sure the verbs are active, not passive. These are three simple changes that will start to give it personality.

CREATE PICTURES. Often, as business writers, we are working with designers. But communication is too important to leave that task only to the designers. We need words that create pictures too, and the process of producing a website, brochure, packaging, poster — any communication — is much more pleasurable if it's a genuine collaboration between writer and designer, between the words and the images. It starts with a conversation. It doesn't matter who takes the lead in this process as long as you come up with a strong idea. The extra weapon that the writer holds is the ability to call upon metaphors, because metaphors are the most powerful way to place vivid pictures in a reader's mind. Words are a colour palette.

8 THINGS TO DO

Look out of the window. Go for a walk. Find an object in the room where you are now. Do any of these things, but use the object you find or something that you see as a metaphor to explain your writer's craft to someone who doesn't consider himself or herself a writer.

SEEK EMPATHY. Nobody likes to listen to monologues, let alone read them. Their message is one of self-absorption. Writing that really works has the character of dialogue, a conversation between writer and reader. When you speak to someone face-to-face, you can gauge their reaction to your words. When you write you don't have that luxury, so you must imagine whether what you say will strike a chord with them or not. You must be able to empathise with them. This may mean telling your readers what they need to hear, rather than what you want to say; and saying it in a way that makes it appealing to them. Make sure that what you write you would also want to read.

7 THINGS TO DO

Imagine you're a playwright. Take something you've recently written at work and rewrite it as dialogue. Use this conversation between two or more characters to get across the original message of your writing.

READING MATTERS. Reading and writing go together. This book has been a demonstration of that relationship, as two writers have read and responded to each other in writing. We both believe that books matter more than ever; in fact they are treasures containing the world's knowledge, wisdom and imagination. We are not in the business of simply conveying information — we aim to do more by engaging with hearts and minds. Reading books helps us to do that. Reading a wide range of books, with a healthy number of novels, poems and stories, is a vital and everyday ingredient in a writer's diet. This applies to the business writer just as much as to the writer of fiction. Writers should treasure books.

6 THINGS TO DO

Choose five books you've read recently (you'll need the actual books). Turn to page 121 of each book, and write down the first line from that page. Using these five lines, or at least elements from them, start writing about a brand or product that you admire.

TELL STORIES. Stories are vital to our wellbeing as humans. Without them our souls wither. Stories help us make sense of the world around us and our place in it. Where facts inform and arguments persuade, stories *involve*. They engage our heads and hearts. They express *a* truth, though not necessarily *the* truth, and they bring people together like nothing else. At work, stories help us make connections — with brands, with each other, with the common purpose, whatever it is. Stories illuminate ideas, heal rifts, solve problems. There's no right or wrong way of telling them and they leave us space to attach our own thoughts and feelings to them. They are, quite simply, the most powerful communications tool we possess.

5 THINGS TO DO

The best story you have to tell is your own. Take whatever time you need to write the first chapter of your autobiography. Where would you start it? What would you call it?

MAKE CONNECTIONS. On one level, writing is simply a matter of connecting one word to another, and then to the next. But it's also about trying to make the best possible connections, the right words in the right order. If you do that, you will achieve a far deeper level of connection between one mind and another. Our contention is that much business writing is actually a disconnection, because it uncouples the natural links in the language of human communication ('Leverage synergy'?!). As human beings we can be almost wilfully open to diversions from objective rationality. It's what we mean when we find communication 'engaging'. Our emotions drive us, in fact they persuade us. And we connect emotionally through storytelling.

4 THINGS TO DO

Reading through the 121 words on *Make connections* above, the word 'random' is not used. Add a word to 'random'. Do it randomly or for reasons of alliteration, eg 'reading', or assonance, eg 'wisdom'. Write about this two-word phrase to describe an aspect of your own writing philosophy.

AVOID ABSTRACTIONS. The trouble is that abstract ideas don't come naturally to us. Children begin telling stories as soon as they can speak, generally around the age of two, but they don't begin to engage with abstract ideas until around eight years old — and then they have to be taught how. 'Leverage synergy', for example, creates no pictures in the mind, triggers no obvious emotions. And that's just two words. A language based on abstractions, as so much modern business-speak is, fails to make the kind of human connection that is essential to all good communication. On the other hand, language that speaks of real people doing real things creates images that lodge more deeply and stays longer in our memories.

3 THINGS TO DO

Make a list of all the abstractions you regularly use at work. Then write your own dictionary definitions for them. Think hard. What do these words really mean for you and the people you work with?

RESPECT CRAFT. You're a writer. Otherwise you really wouldn't have read this book this far. But that's not to flatter you, because we believe everyone has the potential to be a writer. And every writer has the potential to be a better writer. The means to do this are within us all. We can all observe, learn, practise. Never be afraid to take a risk with your writing: always try to push yourself into an area of discomfort, because you'll be developing your own craft as a writer. Analyse what you write: ask yourself if you could write it differently, with another pattern of words to reinforce meaning, with more metaphor or colour, changing structure or rhythm. There's always another way.

2 THINGS TO DO

Try writing without using words that include the letter 'e'. It's an odd thing, forcing you to find words and links you might not normally adopt. Try writing a difficult job application using this method. Then write it again, allowing yourself words with 'e'. What a relief, it's much, much easier. But have you decided to keep any of the writing you produced when you had to think your way around the absence of 'e'?

WRITE ONE-TO-ONE. So here we are, at the beginning again. Everything we've written over the last 51 weeks leads us back to the start — *Room 121*. It's where we meet face-to-face and acknowledge in all the usual ways that we're of the same species, that we're human beings and so we must speak to each other in 'kindness'. When we leave the room, when we're no longer in each other's presence, we must remember its lessons and write as if we were — because not to do so is to submit to the world of Room 101, where language is used to depersonalise, to alienate and to control. We must write one-to-one, person-to-person, human-to-human. It's the best and only way to connect.

… AND ONE LAST THING TO DO

Write a letter to your best friend, telling them everything you can about your work: what you do, how you feel about it, how the people you work with feel about you (and you about them), where it fulfils you, where it falls short and where you would like it to take you.

ACKNOWLEDGEMENTS

We must begin by thanking Stuart Delves for his Introduction to this book; but more especially for his friendship and partnership in the Dark Angels courses we have run together for many years. Then we must also thank all the Dark Angels who have been through those courses, becoming friends and valued fellow writers in the process. We particularly thank those whose words, whether twitter stories or the 'What I love' collective poem, have been reproduced in this book (www.dark-angels.org.uk).

We quote short extracts from other writers in this book and we thank those writers for their words. In particular we thank Elspeth Murray for permission to reproduce her wonderful poem 'This is Bad Enough' in full. You can see her reading it on YouTube.

Business writers cannot write unless they have clients, so we're grateful to those who have commissioned us, and with whom we have enjoyed good relationships as well as creative partnerships. The writers' group 26 needs to be singled out as a fantastic source of support and comradeship for writers, as well as the orchestrator of stimulating creative projects (www.26.org.uk). Often these projects involve working closely with other organisations. We're especially fond of International PEN and the V&A, whose collaborative programmes with 26 are shown in extracts in these pages.

The seasonal photographs dividing the four parts were taken by Jessie Simmons. We openly admit bias but she is a fine photographer (www.jessiesimmons.com). To continue with family matters, love and thanks are due to Linda Simmons and Sarah Jauncey. Without your support, this book would have been impossible to write.

Finally we would like to thank Martin Liu at our publishers Marshall Cavendish for believing in this book, for commissioning it and for steering it through to publication.

John Simmons & Jamie Jauncey
London & Dunkeld, March 2011

ABOUT THE AUTHORS

John Simmons (*right*) and Jamie Jauncey (*left*) are two of the most experienced business writers in the UK. Between them they have written, told stories and trained for businesses and organisations, large and small, in many countries around the world. They are joint founders, along with Stuart Delves, of the acclaimed Dark Angels programme of residential Creative Writing in Business courses (www.dark-angels.org.uk).

Formerly director of verbal identity at Interbrand in London, John is now an independent writer and a director of The Writer (www.thewriter.co.uk). As well as writing, he runs workshops through The Writer and D&AD, and is a trustee of the Poetry Society. His many books include *We, Me, Them & It*, *Dark Angels* and *26 Ways of Looking at a Blackberry*. He has also written three books in the Great Brand Stories series, on Starbucks, the Arsenal and Innocent Drinks. He is a founder director of the national writers' collective 26 (www.26.org.uk).

Over more than 25 years, Jamie's work on the transforming power of language and stories has taken him from boardroom to classroom, library to lecture theatre, training room to conference centre. A founder member of 26 in Scotland, Jamie has published five novels including *The Mapmaker* and *The Witness*, and is also a musician. A former chairman of the Society of Authors in Scotland and member of the Scottish Arts Council's Literature Committee, today he sits on the board of the Edinburgh International Book Festival, the world's largest literary festival (www.jauncey.co.uk).

For more information about John, Jamie and their work, visit their respective blogs at: www.26fruits.co.uk/blog and afewkindwords.blogspot.com

OTHER BOOKS BY THE AUTHORS

 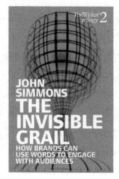 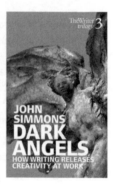

By John Simmons
The Angel of the Stories
Innocent: the inside story of Innocent told from the outside
26 Ways Of Looking At A Blackberry
Dark Angels
The Invisible Grail
We, Me, Them and It

By James (Jamie) Jauncey
The Reckoning
The Witness
The Crystal Keeper
The Mapmaker
The Albatross Conspiracy